From Tears
To Triumph

By Nancy Coleman Carley

And Jesus said, " For
Those Tears I died"

Nancy Coleman Carley

TEACH Services
Brushton, New York

Published by

TEACH Services
Donivan Road
Route 1, Box 182
Brushton, New York 12916

From Tears to Triumph

Lovingly dedicated to
Edward and Mom & Dad

My mom lived to be
97 yrs + 8 mos old before
she died 6/29/01

3

Nancy Coleman Carley

Chapter One

It was Thanksgiving week-end, 1985. Ed was pushing my wheelchair down the side aisle that Saturday morning. When he came to a stop, I moved into the pew praying that I would not fall. I was unaware of anyone watching me.

Between the services, I noticed a lady coming toward us from the opposite end of the pew. She sat down next to me as if I were a friend she hadn't seen in a long time, and started speaking to me.

"My name is Naomi, and I'm visiting from Missouri. When I saw you come in this morning, I told my husband I just have to talk to you; that maybe you could help me...." I was bewildered. What could *I* do for her?

This is her story, told as she wrote it:
I saw this young lady coming down the aisle in the church in a wheelchair, which was being 'motored' (pushed) by her husband. About halfway the chair came to a rest, and she, without help, moved herself out of the chair and into the pew. Her face was bright and cheerful, and with no hint of pain or distress, even tho' it was not without effort that the transition was made. I was just watching her. How long had she been in this crippled condition? What was the problem? My mind immediately went to my younger sister, whom we were visiting in California, along with other relatives. How often we had tried to cheer Sally up, but always the answer

was, "You just don't understand." And surely we didn't! She had been on crutches most of her sixty-odd years of life, having contracted polio when she was only three years old, and being left with only one leg immobile and completely paralyzed. And now her 'good' leg was being affected and her arms were growing weaker, so that she was not able to use the crutches as formerly. It was hard, but God had blessed her with a kind, patient husband, who waited on her hand and foot. Still there was seldom a cheerful word that escaped her lips. A smile was a rare thing. Trying to speak courage to her seemed to only deepen her despair. Then we saw Nancy in Church that day, I thought maybe she might have a thought, a word, a new hope that I might carry to Sally. And so I walked up to the now occupied pew and approached Nancy with my problem. Did she have any answers? Was there some intangible something motivating her that was different from the ordinary Christian believer? Our conversation showed that Nancy had been in that condition a number of years. She, too, had a kind thoughtful husband. Her trust in her Heavenly Father was strong, she knew God loved her and cared for her. And she seemed not to let her mind dwell on the negative side of life, but took an interest in other things. Things she could do, like writing a book and talking with others, sharing her experience. And it all made a difference in her outlook on life, and it showed in her face. The beaming smile, the sparkling eyes, the happy face. There was no distress visible that I saw, and I did not feel afraid to approach her. She encouraged me and I felt better just talking with Nancy.

"Lord, I feel so unworthy, please help me say something that will be of help to her that she can take back to her sister," I silently prayed. She told me that her sister had quit going to church. I felt a heavy burden, as it is only through God's love and our abiding in Him that we can win over our afflictions.

I told Naomi a lot about myself, and how I met Ed. I mentioned my cousin Carol, who had polio when she was four years old, but was younger than Naomi's sister. Also, I mentioned a couple of books which were helpful to me. I still felt I hadn't said much of anything worthwhile, and continued praying for the Lord's guidance in my words. I told her about my parents, and how they were both in their eighties.

"There's something I learned from my Mom recently as she took care of my Dad and his needs. She said she takes one day at a time, and I use the motto now, too." With those words, she went back to sit with her husband. Before she got up to leave she said, "That's something new, I hadn't thought of that. I'll mention that to Sally when we see her again. Thank you very much, you've been a great help."

This lady had given me something priceless; she touched my life with more spiritual healing. If she had approached me ten or fifteen years ago, I'm afraid I would have resented it. How thankful I am that I've grown in the Lord, and He has seen fit to use me in a ministry for Him just as I am.

Mom and Dad met in the Spring of 1922, and on December 27, of that same year they were married.

Tragedy struck the family in August, 1942. Bobby, a brother whom I never knew, died of appendicitis when he was not quite seventeen years old. Penicillin, the 'wonder drug', had been discovered in 1929. It probably would have saved his life, but because World War II was in progress, all the Penicillin was being sent to the war zone to help the soldiers.

Mom and Dad were heart-broken and felt like they could hardly go on living. But there were five other children who needed their love, Harold, Bill, Peggy Ann, Keith and Sharon.

Bobby's death caused Mom's mind to be flooded with questions concerning the state of the dead. She and Dad attended church on Sunday as they sought comfort and answers as to the whereabouts of her second-born son.

One day mom received an answer to her prayers as she picked up the newspaper. The words seemed to leap out at her: "Where are the dead?" A series of meetings were being held in town by Pastor J.R. Johnson.

A great burden was being lifted from her as the evangelist showed from the Bible that the dead are asleep in their graves waiting for Jesus to come.

Never was anyone so excited, as she when she told Dad all about what she had learned. Mom hungered for more and kept attending the meetings. Pastor Johnson also presented the truth about the seventh day being the Sabbath.

My father was beginning to get upset about Mom's newly found truth and had another minister try to "set her straight." Mom was a twentieth-century Daniel, though, and stood her ground. She was baptized into the Seventh-day Adventist Church in 1947. Daddy gave his heart to the Lord in 1950.

My parents were in their early forties when I arrived on October 4, 1944. I was their seventh 'bundle of joy'. I wasn't welcomed by all members of my family though. Sharon, who was only four years old and the baby in the family until I came along, expressed her unhappiness by biting my tiny fingers until they turned blue!

It appeared that I was a normal baby as they looked down into my crib. The thought that one day their baby daughter would have an incurable disease which would cause them and their youngest child many heartaches never entered their mind.

When only a few months old, my health problems began with the chicken pox. Because of a very high fever, I was rushed to the family doctor. The memory of losing Bobby two years before flashed before my parents' minds as Daddy drove the four miles in freshly-fallen snow.

For the next ten years, I was often ill with tonsillitis. Many times it would progress into pneumonia. Penicillin was available now and there were times it no doubt saved my life.

Chapter Two

I felt a lump welling in my throat. My eyes were misty as I walked away. It was the summer that I was eight years old. Mom had taken Sharon and me to Camp Meeting, a place I thought I would have lots of friends. But instead, I found hurt and pain.

The kids my age were calling me "Fly Catcher"! and I didn't know why. I wanted to run. But I just wouldn't let them know how humiliated I felt. Everywhere I went I was called "Fly Catcher." I went out of my way to avoid them.

A few days later when I stepped out of our family tent, I was caught off my guard as two of the children walked by and called out, "Hi, Fly Catcher, did you catch any flies in your mouth today?"

Quickly I stepped back into our tent. Mom was there. She had heard them. It hurt more than ever! Mom tried to comfort me and said, "Don't pay any attention to them."

Those words were so cruel and ugly. When I discovered why I had been given this nasty nickname, I tried ever so hard to make sure my mouth was closed at all times, thinking maybe then those children would not tease me so cruelly any more. (The experience was so painful that for thirty years, I blocked it out of my mind.)

Because my tonsils were so bad, my breathing passages were plugged causing me to breathe through my mouth instead of my nose.

From Tears to Triumph

In October of 1953, shortly after my birthday, we moved to Charleston, West Virginia, where Dad was working because it was hard for him to find employment in Beckley in the mid-fifties. No one wanted to let him have Sabbath off.

Sharon and I had to enroll in different public schools which meant I couldn't go to her for comfort in my confused little world. I didn't want to go to her to whine; she was my anchor, and just knowing she was nearby assured me.

I hated the school that I had to attend. The building was old, ugly, and three stories high. Also, it had the terrible odor of sawdust. The classroom was crowded and I didn't have a desk of my own, so I had to sit on a chair next to a girl who befriended me. I was scared and my eyes were misty, but I didn't want to cry.

I was glad when Friday came. Two whole days of freedom from that smelly school! "How can I ever like it here?" I wondered to myself. "I want to move back to Beckley."

On Monday we enrolled in the Charleston Church School, and once again Sharon and I were in the same school. Miss Bell was not always understanding when I'd miss a few days because of illness. She thought I was twisting Mom around my little finger and was just playing hooky. Sometimes I would like her, other times I resented her for things she did like the time she called me "Nancy Pancy." It was more poignant than it was humorous.

Shortly after my tenth birthday in October, I was sick again with tonsillitis. When Mom and Dad took me to the doctor he said that I should have my tonsils removed.

It was a chilly day in November, 1954, when I entered Charleston Memorial Hospital. I was never more scared in my life than I was as I walked down the hospital corridor. After being given my room and I was clad in a hospital garment, a big, heavy nurse came into my room all smiles. She proceeded with a cheerful conversation and asked questions about myself and my family. She told me she was going to give me a shot. When I laid my head back down on my pillow it wasn't long before my eye lids became heavy and I went to sleep. When I awakened several hours later my tonsils were gone and there was an ice-pack around my neck. I was thirsty and ate ice chips the rest of the day.

That evening when Dad and Sharon came to visit me I was so hungry! I had not eaten since I ate a fried egg and toast at home the night before. I was given all the ice-cream I wanted—and ice-cream was a treat since we didn't have it very often at home—but I was starving for some pinto beans and corn bread served with a tall, cool glass of butter-milk! I wasn't allowed to eat solid foods yet and I couldn't understand why they wouldn't let me have what I wanted. Earlier in the day Dad had brought Mom some of the biggest, juiciest, purple grapes I had ever seen. I begged for some and boy, were they ever delicious! Our family couldn't afford such special things too often.

Next morning I could go home to convalesce and was supposed to keep warm. Mom's idea of keeping quiet and warm was to go to bed! "Now Nancy, you must stay in bed and keep warm so you don't catch pneumonia," she said. I swallowed hard; "PNEUMONIA" was a long word that I couldn't even pronounce. The word should have been familiar to me since I had been sick with it many times in my ten short years of life, but it didn't ring a bell. For some reason I thought it meant something crippling.

I remembered seeing a crippled lady walking. I didn't want to stare, and I didn't, because Mom had taught me, "It isn't nice to stare." "I'm *not ever* going to be like that!" I told myself as I remembered her.

Chapter Three

Sharon had complained often that I walked too slow during the short distances we had to walk each day before and after school. I tried to walk faster, but when I did my side would hurt so much that I could hardly bear it. During the cold winter months when we had to walk a block to the school up a street with a steep incline, the climb was becoming very tiring. The calves of my legs would hurt and I would get out of breath.

One day, thinking it might be less tiring if I went around the block and up to the front of the school rather than enter from the back as we had been doing, I told Sharon what I was going to do. She didn't approve, but I took off on my own anyway.

The calves of my legs still hurt while pumping step after step, and the cold winter air whipped in my face. When I reached the front door of the school after climbing what seemed like a mountain of steps, I noticed no difference from when I was walking up the street. It didn't occur to me that something new was becoming wrong with me, and that I should tell Mom and Dad about it.

In February, 1955, my parents decided to move back to our house in Beckley which had been rented but was now vacant for the last several months. Dad would room at Uncle John's house during the week, and come home for the weekends like he had before we moved the first time. I enrolled in the Beckley Church School.

Just when I started falling down is dim in my memory. It happened sometime during my fourth or fifth year in school. I didn't consider that there was anything wrong until one day while at school I fell down once again for no apparent reason, hitting my knees on the floor. When I tried to get up from a squatting position, I couldn't do it in a normal manner like I had been able to in the past. I had to push myself up by putting my hands on the floor like a baby learning to walk.

"It won't happen again. There's nothing seriously wrong with me; there can't be!" I told myself. I didn't tell Mom about it because I wasn't aware that I should.

Unknown to me, someone else was observing my falls and noticed my walking was not developing normally like the other children my age. Pastor and Mrs. Fralick talked about my problem. They knew something was *seriously wrong*, but they weren't sure what it was. However, they did have a suspicion.

One day Mrs. Fralick mentioned to me her concern about my falling often and asked if my parents were aware of my falls. Timidly I replied, "I guess not." Her asking made me realize for the first time that something could be wrong with me. After school that day when the Fralicks brought me home, Mrs. Fralick said, "Nancy, I'm going in with you so I can talk to your mother."

"Mrs. Coleman, I don't usually interfere in a family matter, but I want to talk to you about Nancy. She's been falling down quite frequently at school and I'm worried that there may be something wrong. There's a possibility that it's Muscular Dystrophy, but I can't say for sure and I don't want to alarm you. There's really very little known about it. A medical doctor from Loma Linda will be at camp-meeting this summer; maybe he can see Nancy.

It was a complete surprise to Mom and Dad that their youngest daughter might have a serious medical problem. After that Mrs. Fralick and Mom asked me to stand up in a door frame. I wondered what that would prove. Mom noticed that my tummy was sticking out and asked me to hold it in. I tried my best to do it, but it wasn't easy. She got a lump in her throat; something *was* wrong.

I was happy-go-lucky, and I still told myself that whatever the problem was, "It won't get any worse."

As time passed though, I *slowly* became weaker. In some ways it was hardly noticeable except for the falls, and my parents observed I was beginning to walk more on my toes. I skinned my knees falling down so many times that I was thankful dresses were long enough (in those days) to keep my injuries covered.

Mom and Dad wanted to seek medical help, but the scarcity of money was a real problem. By the summer I was fourteen I was falling down at least two or three times a month, oftentimes so hard that it jarred my stomach which nearly knocked the breath out of me.

Sometimes I was able to catch myself and prevent a fall. It was terribly EMBARRASSING to fall in a public place. When I did I would always look around to make sure *no one* was staring at me with their mouths hanging open.

My spine was becoming slightly curved, causing my back to start hurting real bad if I stood in one spot for more than five or ten minutes. I didn't complain about the pain I had to endure, and as the years rolled by, I learned to accept that as part of my life—or at least I tried to.

In the summer of 1959, Mom worked at Washington Sanitarium and Hospital in Takoma Park, Maryland, to help with the family finances. She didn't waste any time before checking with several doctors and getting an appointment for me to see one of them.

The doctor, after examining me and making some observations, ordered a complete physical examination to be done at the National Institutes of Health in Bethesda, Maryland. I'm sure he already knew what was wrong, but he wanted a second opinion to be certain. I don't think he wanted to be the one to deliver the bad news to my hopeful mother, either. Fortunately, the waiting period was only a few weeks.

It was a hot, humid day in August, 1959, when I walked into the N.I.H. with my parents. My attitude wasn't much different than the weather. I knew my stay could range from a few weeks to several long months, and knowing how my luck usually ran, I had resigned myself to the latter.

After we had stopped at the admittance desk and filled out the necessary papers, a hospital coordinator led us to the elevator that would take us up to the sixth floor where my room was. After stepping into the already over-crowded elevator, I watched as a nurse pushing a baby crib with a fourteen to sixteen month old baby came in followed by its mother.

The baby's head looked pointed as if the baby had been lying on his stomach from birth with only its head being turned from side to side. There was fluid running from its eyes, nose, and mouth. I looked the mother over critically and wondered to myself, "Why didn't she take better care of her baby?" She was standing over the crib and *seemed* to care. Only she didn't really look like a mother to me with all her make-up and jewelry. The man following her must be her husband, I reasoned, but he didn't seem all that caring about the baby; he only seemed to be concerned about the woman.

The elevator stopped at our floor and startled me back to thinking about my own problems. The coordinator led us down a long hall, around a corner and down another long hall. I was beginning to wish I hadn't worn my three-inch heels. "Nancy," I scolded myself, "why were you so stubborn that you had to act 'grown-up' and wear these high heels, anyway?"

There was very little known about Muscular Dystrophy in those days. I'd heard that it weakened the muscles, but I couldn't picture it ever happening to me, and I'd tucked that bit of information way back in the far corner of my mind.

Saturday morning, after eating my breakfast and watching the rain pour out of the sky, I was wondering how to spend the day. Hospital rules forbade patients from leaving for a few hours, so I couldn't go to church. I was sitting up in my bed still clad in my green baby-doll pajamas when the doctor walked in and interrupted my train of thought. He was followed by one, two, three, four; "A convoy—how many more?" I thought to myself. Altogether, I counted twelve doctors!

I was introduced to each one. It seemed that I was to give the same command performance I had given my doctor five days earlier. That meant off came the top of my baby-doll pajamas again! I hated the idea and felt embarrassed.

"Lift your right leg while lying on your back." (I hadn't been able to lift either leg for several years.)

"Step up on this chair."

"Can you move your arm this way?"

On and on I was tested and tried while each of the doctors made mental notes. It was of very little concern to me if there was something I couldn't do like a normal girl my age.

For another week-and-a-half I was given test after test. During one test seven needles were stuck in my lower right arm at once and I was asked to move a certain finger. As I moved the finger, a television screen showed the movement, and I could hear a popping, cracking sound. It was years before I could stand the sight of a needle again.

Each test was done for a reason and I knew it was useless to ask a lot of questions even if it wasn't much fun. It wasn't much fun to have wires glued to my scalp, either. It took weeks of washing to get all of the glue out of my hair!

After I had been in N.I.H. for almost ten days, the doctor informed me that he wanted to take a piece of muscle from my upper right leg and have it analyzed. I was awake during most of the surgery. I tried in vain to peek and watch the doctor. I could feel every cut numbly, but the nurses had piled the sheets up high in front of me, blocking my view. I was afraid of being scolded if I would move them a wee-bit to see.

I was becoming quite drowsy by the time the surgery was over. When I was taken back to my room, Mom was waiting for me and lunch was being served. On my tray was the biggest submarine sandwich I think I had ever seen. "I'll eat in a few minutes Mom, but first I just want to lie here for a while." When I woke up, supper was being served. I couldn't believe that I had slept for five whole hours instead of only a few minutes.

About one week later on a bright sunny morning, I was already awake and I had a big smile on my face when the nurse came in to take my temperature. I was happy and I didn't even know why. She told me that I was really pretty when I smiled. That made me even more happy and I thanked her. People had commented about my pretty smile before, but when I entered N.I.H., I guess I had forgotten to unpack it with the rest of my belongings until that morning.

A little later in the morning the doctor came by my room and said that I would be released to go home the next day. "Wow, that's great. Thanks!" I said enthusiastically.

The doctor had told my mother a few days earlier that I *did* have Muscular Dystrophy. He told her that I should have a normal life expectancy; in fact I might even outlive her. He said that they should just try to keep me as happy as possible, and I should *never* marry or have any children. I had heard that M.D. was hereditary, so I understood why he said that there shouldn't be any children. What we couldn't understand was where I got it from because, as far as we knew, no one on either side of the family ever had it. One thing I was positive of was that I *wasn't* going to stay single all my life and not marry.

The doctor also told my parents not to take me from doctor to doctor in hopes of finding one that could cure me because there just wasn't any cure. If there had been a cure, Mom and Dad said they would gladly sell our house in order to pay for it. The news of my incurable illness was hard for them to take, but they hid their feelings from me.

Chapter Four

There was still a little warmth left over from summer, even though there was a slight tint of color in the foliage when I entered my freshman year in 1959, at Beckley Junior High School two weeks after the fall session had already begun. The class I dreaded most was gym because my upper legs seemed too skinny to me, and I wasn't at all keen about the idea of taking a shower with the other girls. Since I had been given ten different exercises to do at home for the rest of my life by the physical therapist at N.I.H., I felt fortunate when I didn't have to take the gym class.

I did not know just how Muscular Dystrophy was going to affect my body. Being young and still fairly strong at fourteen, I wasn't able to picture myself as being unable to walk or run someday. Some people said that I might outgrow it, or it would stabilize in my early twenties. How I hoped one or the other could be true. Little did I know about all the heartaches and the hot, salty tears that would spill from my eyes in the times ahead, because I could not foresee the future.

When we got off the bus every morning at school, my classmates would make it to the top of what seemed like a 'zillion' steps leading up to the front door, way before I did. I was always very tired and out of breath by the time I had reached the top. It bothered me more than I wanted to admit that they were able to walk faster than I could, but if I tried to walk any faster, my side would hurt and sometimes I fell before I reached the top.

Since I was a shy person, I didn't have many friends, and I was usually alone at school. I had hoped my cousin Jackie and I would be close pals; however, she had friends of her own and I decided not to be a tag-along cousin. I missed my closest friend Carol, with whom I had attended several lower grades.

I had all the ingredients to keep me from cultivating friendships with other students. I didn't think of myself as being attractive and my big lips bothered me. (When I think about it now, I was attractive, but as a teenager I was very negative about myself.) Also, I had the burden of a speech defect, and I was afraid they would laugh at me.

Sometimes, adults who were strangers to me would tell me that I "couldn't talk plain." Oh, how I wanted to scream at them. I *didn't* need to be reminded. (I had noticed through the years that the ones who were so blunt oftentimes had a speech problem themselves.) I had a hearing deficiency too, which caused problems from time to time. I didn't want a hearing-aid because I had the attitude that they were for old people. Also, they were much larger and more conspicuous than the ones we have now.

By the time I was sixteen, the curve in my spine was becoming more noticeable. It was vexatious because not only did my back hurt more; my clothes didn't look neat, either. I tried to camouflage the curve in my spine so I would look 'normal' by wearing a sweater. Also, I wore my blouses outside of my skirts and slacks rather than tucking them in. These solutions only worked for a little while before I began to notice other problems with my clothes not fitting right.

Because my spine was curving backwards, the more it curved the shorter my blouses were becoming in the front and the back of the blouse was bunched up and didn't look neat at all.

By the time I was eighteen, full skirts were no longer comfortable, and they looked sloppy because the gathers would all bunch around the front while they were pulled flat against the back of my legs.

When I would wake up in the morning and my back was flat against the mattress, I would imagine to myself that I had a perfectly normal figure. But when I would get up and look in the mirror, I would be brought back to cruel reality and the tears would flow. I wanted to believe that something was wrong with the glass, but I knew there wasn't. Full-length mirrors and I soon became enemies.

I had a couple of favorite dresses with full skirts, but soon I had to give them away because the belt would slide below my waist and not stay where it belonged. I even tried pinning the belt to my dress so it would not slide down. I HATED sloppy looking and ill fitting clothes.

Life was becoming *very* frustrating. For a long while I was thinking seriously about committing suicide. At the age of nineteen, I did not feel there was much in life for me to look forward to. Two years earlier, we had visited the Great Falls near Washington, D.C. As I watched the water rushing over the huge boulders, the ugly seed of suicide began to germinate somewhere in the far back corner of my mind. "Why not? How can I make it look like I fell over the railing into the rushing waters by accident?" I asked myself. Then I prayed, "Lord, please help me. What am I thinking?" A volcano of questions erupted in my mind.

My biggest question was, how could I take my own life and not jeopardize my eternal life? Even the thought of killing myself was a sin. Now two years later, I still had not put the thought completely out of my mind. I had conceived a plan where I would take a bunch of sleeping pills at bedtime and get rid of the evidence before falling asleep so no one would ever know what I had done. I wanted my family to believe I died in my sleep. However, God would know. It never occurred to me that my family would want to find out the cause of my death and then they would know, too.

Not long after my thinking those thoughts, Mom came rushing into my bedroom on a sunny August day in 1963, with dreadful news.

"Nancy, your Dad just called from work and said that Mary* shot and killed herself this morning!"

---

*   *Name has been changed.*

"Oh, no Mom, not Mary," I cried, "Why, why....?"

"I don't know honey, I just don't know," she said, as we both cried.

"Mom, she is one of those sincere Christians I admired a lot. It's not fair!"

For days we went about our lives in a daze. I wanted so desperately to turn back the clock, but I couldn't.

Mary's needless death shocked me and affected me in such a way that I knew I wouldn't ever think of committing suicide again, at least try not to, much less act on it. Through God's grace, I knew I would pull out of those deep canyons of depression I fell into from time to time, and go on with life doing the best I could.

My stubborn ego wanted me to be completely like a normal human being. I wanted to learn how to drive a car and I didn't want it to have hand controls, either.

"Nancy, they have hand-controls on cars nowadays. Maybe it would be a good thing for you," Dad had said when I was fifteen. Stubbornly, I closed my ears and made no response to his caring suggestion. He knew he was dealing with a strong-headed daughter, so he wisely dropped the subject.

I had it all figured out. No way would I ever need a car with hand controls. Dad's car had an automatic transmission and that solved all problems as far as I was concerned. My right foot would be for the accelerator only and my left foot would always be in position for the brake. There would be no clutch in the way to be a hindrance to my operating an automobile.

Two years later, when I was seventeen, I came home waving a piece of white paper for Mom to see. I was now a certified, licensed driver and I did it by learning to drive Dad's '57 Dodge with a push-button automatic transmission. Best of all, there were no hand- controls. I had no doubts that I was normal.

My parents encouraged me to be independent and they tried not to smother me by being over-protective. Even still, there were times I felt like they were protecting me more than I liked.

Chapter Five

After I graduated from high school in 1963, I put in a few job applications without any responses. I had hoped to get a job as a dental assistant because I had taken a course in dental assistance as an elective subject in high school. My last two years were taken by correspondence. I wanted to have my picture taken in a graduation cap and gown, and have it on the piano with Sharon's and Peggy Ann's pictures. Since there was no way that could be done when one graduates by correspondence, my cousin Jackie loaned me her cap and gown for a few hours. We were finishing school and graduating at the same time.

I really wasn't trying very hard to get a job because I hated the possibility of being turned down. Very few employers in the 1960's recognized anyone with a physical disability as a potential employee. Another thing that bothered me was the newspaper headlines telling about the millions of people who were unemployed. *"How can I find a job with all those people out of work; I don't stand a chance!"*

My parents had heard about the Rehabilitation office in town which helped the 'disabled' go to college, or sent them to the Rehabilitation Center at an Institute, near Charleston, to further their education or train them for gainful employment.

Exactly what I had expected when I walked into Mr. Hurley's office that day, I didn't know. I did hope, however, that I would be able to take a few classes at Beckley College. Mr. Hurley was 'able bodied' and seemed to think he should handle people like me roughly, as if to teach me a lesson of some kind. It's true I wanted to be treated as a normal human being, but with the cold way he acted, I felt discouraged and only wanted to rebel more. I kept silent and said very little, and I couldn't wait to get out of his office!

When there was an opening at the Rehabilitation Center, they gave me a call. I had known that's where I would be going and not Beckley College. I wasn't happy at all, and I was dragging my feet. I knew I could be there anywhere from six months to a year. Either length of time sounded like an eternity to me!

"Who wants to be with a bunch of people in wheelchairs, and who walk with crutches? I certainly don't," I mumbled to myself.

Mom and dad knew I wasn't very happy about going to the center, but they would talk optimistically, and encourage me the best they could. So I decided to go and try it out, at least.

We were led into an office where they were expecting me, and where we met Susie. She asked us some questions and typed the answers on the form. Susie was in a wheelchair, and smiled as she talked to my parents and me, while she did her work.

"How can she be happy and smile while being in a wheelchair? That smile has to be fake!" I told myself stubbornly.

After Susie was finished, we were ushered into a large waiting room. I looked around enough to see the different types of people who I'd be among for who knows how long. I wanted to get up and leave, but there was nowhere I could escape to. I hated that place!

A center coordinator entered the room. After looking at the chart in her hand, she looked up.

"Nancy Coleman?"

Glad that at last I would be leaving the room full of wheelchairs, crutches, and retarded people, I said, "That's me."

"Would you and your parents follow me, and I'll take you to the dormitory where you will be staying." Dad carried my suitcase and we walked down along the way. She said my room would be on the second floor. She could see how I walked, and thought the stairs might be difficult, so she pointed out the long ramp which led to the second floor.

I wanted to say, "I can walk up steps," but kept silent. She introduced me to the girls dean and some of the girls. Then, taking my suitcase from dad, she led mom and me to the room where I would be living. There were six beds in one large room, but the room was divided up nicely with each girl having a unit four by six feet which had four drawers, a mirror, and a place to hang clothes. But there didn't seem to be enough light in the rooms, and they could stand a good coat of paint. The windows looked like they could stand a good washing to remove what looked like several years accumulation of dirt. Mom and dad left, and I wanted to cry. *"Too big for that now,"* I thought.

Pam was one of my roommates, and she was telling me all the rules, helping me to fit in. She was an orphan, and had been at the Center for almost a year. Supper was about ready to be served as Pam led me to the cafeteria. I wondered why there were two lines, but I didn't ask. Soon it became obvious that one of them was for the people in wheelchairs and using crutches. *"That is the one line I intend to stay out of,"* I said to myself as Pam and I got into the other line, which was for those who were able to walk on their own. We had to stand in line for five or ten minutes, and my back was starting to hurt from standing still. It didn't bother me when I walked, unless it was a long walk.

Inside the cafeteria I discovered the real reason for the two lines outside in the hall. The ones in wheelchairs and the ones on crutches had a special table where they went and took their places, because they couldn't carry their trays of food. It was brought to them by some workers who were in training at the center.

I felt a tightness in the pit of my stomach. I could manage with something small and light in one hand, but not in both hands at the same time. I asked Pam in a whisper if she would carry my tray to the table, which she did. One of the helpers noticed I was new and couldn't carry my tray and said, "The ones who can't carry their trays are supposed to sit at that table," pointing to the one with all the wheelchairs and crutches. Since Pam had already taken my tray to the table of what I called 'mostly normal' people, she didn't make a big deal out of it, only mentioning that I should sit at the other table when I came for breakfast in the morning.

The next morning I had other ideas if I could get away with it. I thought to myself, *"If Pam or someone else was willing to carry my tray, why couldn't it be that way?"* I was noticed when I came into the cafeteria before I got two feet inside the door and one of the workers led me to the table I dreaded! I got as far away from the crutches and wheelchairs as I possibly could, and sat by myself. It was lonely sitting with no one to talk with or listen to.

Every morning at five-thirty, the bell rang for everyone to wake-up and get dressed for breakfast. "I hate getting up at five-thirty in the morning!" I mumbled grumpily to myself. Some rules I didn't mind, but that one I resented. After a few days I discovered that if I didn't mind missing breakfast, I could sleep in at least an hour longer. I didn't eat breakfast at home, so I didn't mind at all missing it there. After all, it was one less meal I'd have to sit at the table with all the wheelchairs and crutches.

I had a lot of growing up to do, but my biggest problem was that I was suffering from *very low* self-esteem.

To find out what kind of job I would be best suited for, they put me in a diagnosis training program. I was tested in different areas: typing, filing, math, sewing, and others. I didn't try my best in some of the areas, because my low self-esteem caused me to think I couldn't do it very well, anyway.

I made it through the first week. In the evenings, I got acquainted with more people, and could feel comfortable being with them. I had even gone over to the recreation center and played ping-pong, which was one of my favorite games to play.

I shyly walked over by the table and sat down to watch. The girl sitting in a wheelchair asked my name, and if I'd like to play. Betty, I discovered, graduated from high school with my sister, Sharon. I felt a little kinship toward her. I hadn't seen her at the table where I sat in the cafeteria, and wondered why.

There were four of us playing ping-pong, so we played doubles. Betty and her 'normal' boyfriend played against Jack, who had only one leg, and me. I didn't know how he lost his other leg, so

I reasoned to myself that he lost it in the Vietnam war. He laid his crutches aside, and hopped around on the one leg to play. When the ball went too far, I went chasing after it. It pleased me that I could move around with so much ease. I couldn't see myself as a handicapped person. Betty played well in her wheelchair, and so did Jack.

"I wish I knew how to fit myself in, but I'm always afraid that if I walk up to someone and start talking they will walk away, and my words will hang in mid-air with no place to land," I thought to myself.

I avoided drinking any water, because I knew how horrible it tasted. But one day it was so hot that I got quite thirsty and gave in. *"Ugh! This water tastes as bad as it did ten years ago when we lived near here. Maybe even worse,"* I said to myself as I drank some more while holding my nose. Fifteen minutes after drinking the water I burped. The horrible chemical taste came back into my mouth. A day or two later I noticed that the chemicals in the water had caused me to break out in hives!

They put me in more diagnosis training the second week. I wondered about a lot of things, but was too shy to ask questions. There was some construction going on at the center, and I got a hint that that was where I might be best suited for training, when it was finished. It could lead into the field of computers. I liked that field, or working in a dental office. I wondered why they weren't helping me in that area. I got the impression they didn't think I could handle that type of job. I knew I could do that job, but most dental offices at home were on the second floor.

One afternoon in the second week, they gave me some math to do. I wondered what that would prove. Before the teacher left the room, he looked at me straight in my eyes and said, "It's a *very cruel world* out there, and there will be many hard knocks. You don't know what you're in for...." I felt intimidated and my eyes were burning. He was making me feel guilty about something, and I knew I hadn't done anything. Finally, he left the room. I didn't try to do my best with the math problems; I really didn't care after the mean way he spoke to me.

There were only three others in the room, with me being the only girl. I kept quiet as I always did, but Charlie, who was blind, was kidding around a lot. He amused me, and in a way, he was helping me to come out of my shell without realizing it. Charlie wanted to know what I looked like. Telling him the best I could about myself, I said, "I have light brown hair, blue-green eyes, I'm five feet five, and I'm nineteen years old." He wanted to come over to me and 'see' me. I had had a perm put in my hair only a week before coming to the center, and it was a little coarse with tight curls. He told me he thought I was a pretty girl.

In a little while he wandered out of the room. After a few seconds, we heard some girls down the hall squealing. Charlie had gone to the rest room, but miscounted the doors and wandered into the girls rest room by mistake.

"Don't worry girls," he told them, "I didn't see a thing!"

Charlie told me that he lost his sight in the army. I liked his sense of humor, and he made the place seem not so bad, after all.

I caught a bus on Friday evening and went home for the week-end. I was trying to make the best of my stay at the Rehabilitation Center with the hopes that six months would pass quickly! I was learning to fit in.

I returned on Sunday evening. Monday morning, when I went to see where they were going to put me that week, they told me that they thought I would do best in training when the new unit was finished. I knew in my heart that I'd do the best I could as long as I was there, but *no way* would I return later. I was given a bus ticket, and I went back to the dorm to pack my things. I carried my suitcase down the stairs and to the double glass doors of the main building. The stinking smell of stale cigarette smoke that saturated the place slapped me in the face as I opened the door one last time.

Even though smoking was not allowed in the buildings, the stale odor was there. I would hold my breath for as long as I could when I came in from the outside, then the terrible odor would go up my nose and to my throat, and I felt like I was choking. Cigarette butts dotted the sidewalks outside the buildings. Many didn't seem to know or care what the sand buckets were for, even though the buckets were conveniently placed. I was glad I wouldn't have that stinking odor to endure any longer!

I wanted to say good-bye to Charlie, but I didn't know where to find him, and I needed to hurry so I wouldn't miss my ride to the bus station.

A number of months later Mr. Hurley called me from his office in town. He told me the new addition was finished, and I could go back to the Rehabilitation Center. I told him that I did not want to go. He wasn't at all happy, but I didn't care.

My parents weren't too happy with my decision, either, and they tried to encourage me a little. But they could see I had made up my mind and decided to abide by what I wanted to do.

Not long after I returned home from the Rehab Center, I received a letter from someone in a nearby town. Looking at the return address, I was puzzled. I knew that I didn't know this person as I opened the envelope. "Dear Nancy, I want to invite you to join in the fun and games for the handicapped...."

"HANDICAPPED!" I said to myself furiously. *"You've got to be kidding?"* I skimmed through the rest of the letter for the sake of courtesy.

"Nancy, who's your letter from?" mom asked.

"Nothing important," I mumbled as I got up from the couch and went to my bedroom and closed the door. I ripped the letter into a dozen pieces and threw it in the waste basket as if it were dirt.

"How dare that person, whoever she is; I'm...I'm...not h...! I have no intentions of going somewhere to be around another bunch of people on crutches or in wheelchairs!" I stubbornly told myself.

A month went by and I received another letter. I recognized the penmanship— it was very neat. I opened the envelope and unfolded the three or four pages (she wrote long letters). After reading a few lines, my blood started to boil again!

Without reading further, I ripped the letter on the spot. *"Who does she think she is, anyway?"* I was getting more angry inside, but I kept it to myself.

Another letter came after several month went by. This time I didn't even bother to open it. I simply ripped it to shreds and threw it in the waste basket. *"Is she ever going to give up?"* I wondered. A few more letters came, and I did the same thing with them. The sender finally got the message that I didn't *ever* intend to 'join in on the fun and games for the handicapped'.

Chapter Six

Because I was self-conscious of the way I walked and stood, I was living in a small world of my own, seldom going out to public places other than to church. Whenever I needed something from the store, I usually asked mom or dad to get it for me.

"I wish you and your mother would go shopping. Every time I go for you, there's always something wrong with what I get," dad said impatiently when I asked him to pick up a pair of nylons for me.

"Maybe he's right. Since mom doesn't know how to drive, I'll take her and she can get my personal items. That way I won't have to get out of the car and it should solve the problem," I said to myself.

A few days later, I took mom to town to do some shopping for herself and me. I tried to tell her what I wanted and the correct size. She went in while I waited for her in the car. When she returned, I checked to make sure that what she had bought for me was what I needed. Unfortunately, it was all wrong! Mom patiently returned to the store to make an exchange. While she was gone, I had some time to think about what was happening. *Is this what I want for the rest of my life; Mom and Dad doing my shopping when I have two legs that are capable of walking just about anywhere I want to go?* The thick layers of self-pity and self-consciousness began to slowly peel away. *I'm not going to let people's stares run or ruin my life. I will do my own shopping.*

I had gone to J.C. Penney's to look for a dress that would be comfortable and look neat on me. After what seemed like hours of going through rack after rack, I went home empty-handed and my back aching terribly, to cry my heart out in Mom's loving arms. "Mom," I cried, "I looked and looked and there's nothing I can wear. What am I ever going to do?"

Mom had made most of Sharon's and my dresses when we were growing up. She always made mine too wide. I was growing up, not out.

It never occurred to me to seek God in prayer for an answer. I thought I had to be the one to find a solution. No doubt, though, He did look down with tender love, showing me where to find my answers even without my ever realizing it till years later.

Since the Spiegel catalog had been a part of our family for a number of years, I would always go through each new one when it arrived at our house in the mail to explore what was new and with the hope of finding something that I could wear.

When I was twenty-one a new style came out which I wanted to try. A sale catalog came which had a pretty red knit outfit with a straight skirt and a tunic top. I reasoned that the skirt had no gathers to fall around the front and a tunic top was longer than other blouses. Mom did not think it would look neat on me, so it took a little to persuade her. We ordered it and when it came, it fit perfectly and was comfortable! It became my favorite best dress for several years. *If only I could order any dress I liked and each one would fit perfectly, that would be the end of my frustrations with clothes.*

That did not end my search for perfect fitting clothes. After several years had passed, the red dress no longer looked nice on me. My back was swaying backward more and it looked awful. I was learning to sew and through many trials and errors, I would finish something only to give it away. It didn't matter that I couldn't climb trees or jump rope anymore, but it did matter very much to me how my clothes looked. Oh, how I longed for that perfect figure I had in my early teens, and the favorite princess-style dress I had worn.

Quite often one summer, whenever I came home from an outing, I would quickly put on my yellow duster. "At least I don't feel or look too bad, considering," I reasoned to myself. My niece, Christine, who was a year-and-a-half younger than me and married, wanted to know why I was wearing the duster so much.

I thought to myself, "How could she ever know or understand how I feel, and the frustrations I have with clothes? After all, hers fit so neatly." I just told her it was more comfortable to wear the duster, and left it at that.

I disliked being around people who did a lot of complaining. I still had battles with depression from time to time. Sometimes it would last three or four weeks and usually was brought on by something someone said about my physical handicap or walking. I often wondered why parents did not teach their children what Mom had taught me as a small child even before anyone suspected that one day I would have a physical disability. She had taught me, "Don't stare, it isn't nice," and "Don't ask questions." Even adults were guilty of making candid remarks as if they had never seen or heard of anyone who walked differently than they did. Sometimes children would try to mock the way I walked and that really hurt!

I wondered why people couldn't look at me and realize that I am just as human as they are? Many people think that if you are physically handicapped, you are mentally deficient, too.

When the fog of depression lifted, I could laugh and had quite a sense of humor. The Lord has so many ways of helping, but the trouble was, I often could not understand when there were so many trials in my way. He had promised He would not let us go through more than we can bear. Sometimes, when I felt like I had had all I could endure, I pleaded, "Lord, please let me die!"

"Lord, if all things work together for good to them that love You... how come You don't heal me so I can tell others about Your great love? I'm not strong enough to help You as I am," I asked.

Chapter Seven

Just like any other young woman, I desired to get married and have a home of my own, and prayed about it many, many times. As time passed by and that didn't happen, I began to feel like either God was not listening to my prayers or He must not love me as much as He did other people.

At a very young age, I developed a crush on two fellows. One of them was Tommy, who attended the same church I did and the other was Bobby, who lived a short distance from us. Our older sisters were good friends. Bobby was a very sincere Christian of another faith. I hoped that some day I would marry one of them. I noticed that Tommy never seemed to notice me whenever I was close to him but Bobby did. In the end I knew it was Bobby I wanted to marry.

When I was in the third grade and Bobby was in the fourth, we were in the same class room. One day after school Sharon told me teasingly, "Agnes said Bobby likes you." It made me feel good. Even though we hardly spoke more than a few words to each other, I always felt protected when he was nearby. When I was in the seventh grade and he was in the eighth, we were in the same classroom again.

When I was in the ninth grade, Bobby and I rode on the same school bus, but we attended different schools. He went to Woodrow Wilson High School and I went to Beckley Junior High. Bobby would smile at me when he got on the bus and soon he started sitting beside me as we rode to and from school. I liked to have him sit by me, but I was terrified that I would blush or say something dumb and he would laugh at me and stop liking me. I could not handle the situation very well. We were too young to get serious, so we remained merely good friends.

I didn't like his pimples. In fact, they turned me off. It never occurred to me at the time that they were only temporary. I wasn't feeling very well because the Muscular Dystrophy was reprogramming my body.

So, one day I decided to be less friendly to Bobby. He had given me a recent school picture of himself only a few days before. When I got home, I tore it up along with the one he had given me in the seventh grade. Later on, I truly regretted my hasty action, because then I didn't have a picture to look at and dream of him. I only had my memories to rely on. Poor Bobby never knew why I suddenly turned cold toward him, and I didn't even know how to explain it. Finally, he stopped sitting by me. I couldn't bear to look at him, because I knew I had hurt him badly.

Since we moved again, we didn't see each other for nearly a year. In the meantime, I realized that I did like him a lot and thought how silly I had been. I had the opportunity nearly a year later to go to his house to pick up some eggs. (His mother raised chickens and sold eggs.) When his mother went to get the eggs, she told Bobby that I was there. My heart fluttered in my chest as he came into the room. There he stood, one arm behind his back with his hand holding the other arm at the elbow. And there was that shy smile that he had always had *just for me*. He walked me to the door when it was time to leave. I wanted to talk more, but I was afraid I was blushing and he could hear my heart doing somersaults in my chest. It was nearly Christmas so we wished each other a "Merry Christmas" and I didn't see him again until he graduated from high school one-and-a-half years later.

My cousin Charlotte was graduating at the same time Bobby was and obtained a ticket for me to attend the graduation ceremony. She thought I wanted to go because she was graduating, but secretly I was going to see Bobby, and I hoped I would get a chance to say "Hello."

I spotted him among the two-hundred graduates. I wanted to speak to him after the ceremony, but I was a little apprehensive, too. *Would my having M.D. bother him?* (It had progressed and was more noticeable now.) *Would it cause him to turn cold toward me?* I went home disappointed because I couldn't find him in the huge crowd afterward.

Now that we were older, I had high hopes that Bob would stop by the house to see me or call asking for a date. Mom mentioned one day, "Bobby went by the house a little while ago." Perplexed, I asked how she had seen him and I didn't.

"I was cleaning the bedroom windows and he waved as he rode by on his bike."

A few other times Mom saw him again and so did Dad. *How come they see him and I don't? And why doesn't he stop to see me?*

I learned from them that he seemed to ride by on his bike around three o'clock. I began to search through my thoughts and came up with an idea I thought would be fun. It had worked for Mom and Dad; maybe it would work for me, I reasoned.

With a twig of birch in hand, I went out on our front steps and took off my shoes a good while before three o'clock. I thought it would be exciting to meet Bob again the same way Mom and Dad had met for the first time; barefoot and chewing on a birch twig on the front steps of our home.

I had kept quiet about my plans because I knew how Dad loved to tease, especially when it came to boys. That always embarrassed me and I hated it. Bob never came by that day and I gave up my fanciful idea. Two years went by.

In the 1960's, it was not popular, or even proper, for a girl to ask a boy for a date. Even if it had been, I still would never have done it. Sharon, who was with us along with her children for a few weeks while her husband, John, was in Florida holding meetings, suggested that we ask Bob if he would like to play miniature golf with us.

"But isn't that like asking him for a date?" I asked.

"No," she said. She knew how much I wanted to see him, so I went along with her idea since mine never seemed to work.

When we arrived at his house, I felt terrified. I expected Bob's eyes to light up and he would have that special smile for me. I was disappointed when he hardly looked up from the needle-work he was doing to say a simple "Hi." He declined to play miniature golf with us. Such a let-down.

Several months later, I decided to stop by his house to visit with his mother. Before we had talked for very long she said, "I guess you won't ever be getting married because you can't have any children." Those words struck out at me like a sharp knife stabbing into my heart and the tears stung in my eyes. I wanted to cry out at her, "What's not having children got to do with my getting married?!" I was not going to humiliate myself by crying there for her to see, so I quickly made an excuse why I had to be on my way, and left.

As I drove home, the tears burned as they trickled down my cheeks and splattered into my lap. I realized then that she must have told Bob I would be a helpless person for the rest of my life (or something like that), and that's why he never stopped at my house to see me. I have no doubt, now, that she didn't mean to be cruel; however, it took a decade before I could share the humiliation I suffered that day with my mother.

It wasn't long after that I spotted him with his arm around someone else. As soon as I was alone, I cried my heart out.... *"Oh Lord, why? I thought You meant him for me."* He was melting out of my life, and there didn't seem to be any hope of a future with him.

Only a short time later I saw his engagement notice in the newspaper. My dreams had been shattered, and there wasn't a flicker of hope left. With the Lord's divine help, I was able to get on with my life.

Chapter Eight

It was always painful for Mom and Dad when I would fall. But the falls weren't as hard for me to bear as was the wretched expressions on their faces. When I would take a spill as a child, I would offer a child-like excuse. When I got older, it seemed like the best medicine to ease the pain of a hard fall was to laugh.

One day while I was walking with dad from the garage to the house, I fell down even though I was holding on to his arm. A couple of times in the past I had even pulled him down with me. Fortunately we had always been able to laugh about it and that would ease the tension. But this time it upset him so much that he cried out in anguish, "Oh why does God allow this?" I wanted so much to tell him that it wasn't God's fault I had fallen, but the words got hung up in my throat.

We knew that sin in the world was responsible for all the heartaches we humans have to endure, and I didn't blame God and Dad didn't either. It's just that he felt so helpless because there was nothing in this world he could do to help his youngest daughter. He could only watch her grow weaker and weaker year after year.

I always liked the extra humor my brother-in-law, Sharon's husband John, added to my falls. He would spice up my falls by saying, "Nanny, what's ya been drinkin'?" There was never a 'pity' or "Are you hurt anywhere?" routine from John. He made me feel like nothing out of the ordinary had happened.

My ego got crushed whenever I would fall down in a public place. I had always hoped and prayed that I would never fall in church, but unfortunately I did fall there three times. The first time was when I was fifteen and church had just gotten over. I was wearing the highest pair of high-healed shoes I ever owned. I could feel my cheeks growing red with embarrassment as I struggled to get up. Some people had said that I should not be wearing high-heeled shoes lest they might cause me to fall. I wanted to scream! I had fallen a 'million' times in the past when I was wearing flats. Why didn't they just tell me I had better go barefoot?

The second time I fell was when I was visiting Sharon and John where John pastored a church in Big Stone Gap, Virginia. I had walked up to the piano to play for Sharon because she was going to sing for the special music with me as the accompanist. My two-and-a-quarter inch heel got caught in the loose edge of the runner carpet. Before I had time to realize what had happened, John had come to my rescue and helped me up. He knew just how to put his arms under mine to lift me up, and the whole incident was taken care of as if it had never happened.

The third time was when I was about twenty-four. It seemed like each fall was spaced about five years apart. I had just finished teaching my Primary Sabbath School class and I was walking to the second pew from the front of sanctuary when I fell down so hard I could hear the floor jar. And it was right in the front of the church just before the service was about to begin, of all places!

Before I knew what was happening, two strong men were there to rescue me. Dad had risen to his feet when he saw me fall and started down the aisle. I had fallen so many times since I was ten years old, by now I had learned to endure it. When I reached the second pew where I wanted to sit, the minister, Pastor Knoll was sitting on the third pew. As I sat down, Pastor Knoll leaned over and whispered in my ear, "If I preach too long, fall again, O.K.?" With a laugh, I said I would.

Since I was a small child, I tried to maintain a close relationship with God. I was baptized when I was ten. Five years later, I noticed a book Mom had called "ESCAPE FROM DEATH," by

Roy and Rose Slaybaugh. I asked her what the book was about. The picture on the cover had captured my attention: a woman was by the bedside of her husband who was all bandaged up.

The story was about a couple who were converted to the Adventist faith and had a burning desire to do missionary work for the Lord. One day in 1945, Roy Slaybaugh was involved in a terrible automobile accident, caused by two teenagers who were running from the law. At the hospital, Mrs. Slaybaugh was told her husband had a compound fracture of the skull and cerebral fluid was draining out of the left eye and ear with no way to stop it. The doctor expected him to die at any minute. Mr. Slaybaugh also had a broken jaw, one ear was cut off, and the sight in his left eye had been destroyed.

Someone suggested to Mrs. Slaybaugh that she should call in the elders of the church to pray for her husband and anoint him. It had been three days since the accident and he was near death. After the prayers and the anointing, Mr. Slaybaugh recovered; even his ear that had been cut off healed with only a scar left as a reminder of the accident.

As I read the story, I drank in every word. It was the first time I had become aware that Jesus still heals as He did two thousand years ago when He walked on the earth. I had heard of the faith healers on television, but I didn't believe in them.

After reading James 5:14-15 a number of times, it became a favorite text of mine. I began to toy with the idea of asking for anointing for myself. I knew that when we ask God for something, we are supposed to ask for it to be according to His will. I did not understand a great deal about God and how He works at that young age. Nonetheless, I did know I wanted to be healthy and STRONG. Pastor Johnson came to anoint me in the summer of 1960, and I was happy to let God's will be done. In the back of my mind though, I really was hoping and expecting God to rid my body of Muscular Dystrophy. No matter how hard I tried to remember that God said He would never leave or forsake us, (Hebrews 13:5) sometimes I felt like He had let me down because I was not healed. Many times I wondered why God was letting me grow weaker instead of my getting stronger. I didn't realize at the time that I would be spending many years in God's classroom before I would understand.

When I was seventeen, I had started up the front steps of our house and fell near the top. I had no reason to think I might fall because I had walked and even run up and down the ten steps since I was five years old. When Dad saw me falling, he rushed to catch me. In his arms, I sobbed, "Dad...I can't walk up these steps any more without falling."

In my early twenties, I could still walk up and down steps if there was a hand-rail on each side of the steps or I could hold onto the arm of someone on my left side. My parents had remodeled the kitchen with the outside door and steps moved. Before Dad got the new rails put up, he helped me go up and down them even though there were only four steps.

Dad was curious how I got up the steps when he wasn't around to help me. He knew I had done it several times, but he didn't know how I did it, and I wasn't interested in telling him how, because I was very self-conscious. I always made sure no one was watching when I went up them alone. I even made sure no cars were passing by the house because I didn't want anyone's pity or staring, watching how abnormally I did it.

Then one Saturday afternoon, I decided to take a drive in the car since it was a beautiful day. When I returned, I assumed my parents would be taking a nap. After putting the car in the garage, I walked across the lawn to the back steps. I put my right foot on the first step, then my right hand on that knee. Next, I put my left hand on a step further up for balance followed by raising my left foot onto the first step. It was one step at a time. When I got to the top step, I walked the few feet to the door, opened it, and there stood Dad!

He said that he had started to come out to help me only to decide to stay in the background out of sight to see how I got up the steps when I was alone. I was irritated with him for watching me struggle, but he seemed proud that I could do it, so I didn't stay angry for very long.

What was this the minister was saying about Divine Healing? I can't say what his exact words were that summer Sabbath morning. He was talking about how we as Christians could study THE MINISTRY OF HEALING (by Ellen G. White) and apply its words of wisdom to our life and we could receive Divine Healing.

As I read the story of the woman who had suffered twelve years from an affliction which made her life a burden, my mind soaked it in like a sponge even though I already knew the story by heart since childhood. The woman had gone from physician to physician spending all her money, but she had not been healed. She heard about Jesus and His wonderful healing power. She decided to go where He was. Rather than bother Jesus because of the large crowd around Him she thought to herself, "If I may touch His clothes I will be made whole." So she touched His clothes and she was healed.

But..., Jesus isn't on earth now like He was two-thousand years ago, so how could His healing power be for me? I pondered over the fact that I had been anointed seven or eight years earlier. Does it mean that when we ask Jesus for something, we are to continue asking for healing, or anything else we may desire for that matter?

It was exciting to think of being healed. I could go buy a dress and it would fit. I could have dates and get married. I went on and on about all the things I would do. Then a thousand other questions came rushing into my mind. One of the main questions was, if a guy doesn't like me now the way I am, why should he have me when I'm healed and strong? I wanted someone to love me for me. That way I would always know he would stand by my side no matter what happened.

"Lord," I prayed, "I do want to be healed, but I'd like to wait until after I'm married and talk to You more about this."

With that, I put healing on hold with the hope of not getting any weaker in the meantime.

Chapter Nine

The September landscape was dotted with orange, red, and gold. The air was cool and rain lightly falling as we drove home after Dorcas' wedding. (Dorcas, who is my oldest niece, is five months older than me.) One part of me was thrilled for her and her sister Christine who had married two years earlier, but another part of me was hurting. There was a bit of self-pity under my skin which was crowding my thoughts of happiness because I wasn't yet married, and I had no prospect of ever finding a husband with whom to share my life.

Apparently, it seemed to me, Dad didn't even think I would be getting married one day. While we were all eating dinner before the afternoon wedding, he had remarked to Harold, "You'll soon have three sons-in-law like I do" (Jeanie was planning a December wedding.)

The words crushed my heart into a million pieces and brought tears to my eyes. *"Daddy, you have four daughters, not three!"* I wanted to scold. (Dad was a widower with a daughter named Nellie when he and Mom were married.) I wanted to run someplace and cry, but the bedrooms were all upstairs and I could no longer spontaneously run or walk up and down them anymore. When I did have to climb stairs, it was slowly, one step at a time, so I just sat there. Quietly I dabbed the mist from the corner of my eyes with fingers and pasted a false smile on my face.

Several years later when I mentioned the incident to him he apologized. "I'm so sorry, honey, that I hurt you. I didn't even know you wanted to get married someday." He liked to tease me sometimes, but I wasn't always fond of his bantering so I had hidden my desires from him as long as I possibly could. When we did talk about my marrying he said, "There's always someone for everyone, and there will be someone for you."

Dad and I were very close and I felt like I could talk to him about almost anything. Because Mom would cry so easily when she saw me hurting, I would usually go to Dad. I knew he would be strong and comfort me. I felt bad when I cried in front of Mom because then she would start crying too, and I would end up trying to comfort her.

One day I asked Dad the question, "If Mom had had a physical problem, would you have married her?" I don't know what I expected him to give for an answer. Perhaps I was looking for an answer giving me hope. "Well honey, I've never thought about that. I'm not sure what I would have done."

Although my nieces and I had grown up together like sisters and were very close, neither of them had asked me to be in their wedding. *"Why couldn't they have at least given me the benefit of the doubt and asked me?"* I thought to myself, *"I would have declined."* It really hurt because they didn't at least ask. Dorcas, however, was more considerate. She ordered a corsage just for me. "Because you couldn't be in the wedding." she said.

Being in either wedding would have meant having my picture taken while I was standing up, and I couldn't bear the thought of that. I would always sit down when my picture was being taken so that I would 'look normal'. But I would have loved to help with the receptions, at least. It never occurred to anyone that I could take part in the weddings by sitting on a stool while being in charge of the guest book or refreshments.

It was a beautiful spring Sabbath, and another winter was in the past. I was sitting in church only half listening to the sermon. My thoughts were preoccupied with wishing and praying for something to do in the church so I could be more useful. I was afraid to tell anyone that I would like something to do for fear they would only say something like, "What can you do?" or, "You aren't strong enough." Oftentimes, someone with a physical disability is considered useless or in the way, and is treated as such, (for their own good, of course).

The Lord knew what was in my heart and heard my prayers. Before long, Opal asked if I would play the piano for the Primary Division Sabbath School class. I made a feeble protest, because I knew I wasn't very good, but she insisted that I play for them. "Just do the best you can," she said.

Most of the music was easy to play, but I still made my share of mistakes. Opal would merely smile and keep on singing.

A few weeks later she gave me a story to tell. I *loved* the idea of telling stories, but I worried about my speech. The words all sounded perfect to me and no one else said anything, so maybe God corrected it, as I requested. God was leading me.

Working with Opal and the children was a joy and I was thankful someone believed in me. Soon ideas of how to make the classroom more attractive were swimming around in my mind. I changed the room around to look more appealing to the children. I had an idea that I just couldn't resist and I asked Opal for her permission to do it. When she said "yes," I went on with my plans. I remembered going to Sabbath School one morning when I was five years old and seeing paper birds 'flying' on a string across the ceiling. I wanted to share with these little ones the same thrill and memories I had. Of course, I got teased about going back into my second childhood.

I had a room full of blessings; that is, until one Sabbath when a young lad walked in. His name was Ronnie. "Lord," I cried, "Why did You send him here?" When I saw Ronnie, I was reminded of myself. I had not yet accepted my Muscular Dystrophy and I certainly could not accept anyone else who might have a physical problem. I didn't want to be around anyone who did!

There it was again; the heavy thump-thump sound as Ronnie was walking down the hall into the classroom each Sabbath morning. I could not bring my eyes to look at him for several weeks. I knew he must feel self-conscious about the thick-soled shoes with braces. He was born with a birth defect, I decided. I was thankful I didn't have wear a brace of any kind. Then, one Sabbath morning it happened. I don't recall how it happened, it just did. I noticed Ronnie's beautiful blue eyes and his million dollar smile. Oh, how I fell in love with him. I was taking another step in the right direction. I was learning to accept others with physical problems.

My mind flashed back to when I was eleven. The rain had washed the earth clean and the summer sunshine had reappeared. Company had pulled up and stopped in front of our house that Sunday afternoon. I didn't remember ever having seen them before, but my parents seemed to know who they were. My attention was focused on the little six-year-old boy. His legs and feet were twisted and he struggled to walk while his mother held both of his arms to help him walk across the lawn and up the front steps. "That father is cold-hearted; why doesn't he help?" I wondered. Sharon apparently thought the same as I did. Later on, I found out the man was the boy's stepfather.

While Mom, Dad, Sharon, and I sat in the living room to visit with them, thoughts were tumbling around in my head faster than I could keep up with.

"Maybe I do fall down, but I'm never going to be like that. After all," I reasoned, *"Whatever is causing the falls will go away like a cold. Besides, my limbs are all normal and not twisted, so how could I ever be crip—?"* (I never did like that word and it always got hung up in my throat.)

When the visitors got ready to leave, Sharon hopped to her feet and said, "Let me help you with the little boy." I couldn't believe my ears; did I hear right? Sure enough, she got on one side of the little boy and helped while the mother was on the other side. "Sharon, how can you do such a thing; I know I couldn't," I thought to myself with my nose turned up in the air. I was glad as I watched her that she had compassion for people, (much more than I did, I'm afraid.) I wanted to hug her and tell her, "Sharon, I'm so proud of you. You're really special!"

Chapter Ten

All of my friends had married; most of them to non-Adventists. I wanted to marry someone of my own faith, but how could I do that when all the single males in the small Beckley Church were gone? *"Maybe I'll have to do what Sharon did, convert my husband to my own faith. It didn't seem so hard for her,"* I reasoned. Sharon had met John during their senior year of high school. John was planning to study to become a Baptist minister after he graduated. One thing I had forgotten was all those tears and a break-up in the meantime. All that I was thinking about was that they were married in August, 1958, and he went on to school to become an Adventist minister.

During the Spring of 1969, I saw an ad in the "Family Weekly" section of the Sunday newspaper. An advertisement for a "Computer Dating Service" captured my attention. I had seen the ad a number of times before. I wanted to give it a try, but on the other hand, I was terrified to do it. What would people think, especially Mom and Dad? But this time when I noticed the ad, I got enough courage to ask Sharon what she thought about it.

"Do it!" she said.

"You're kidding?"

"No, do it. It will be fun."

"But what.... OK, I'll do it!" I was relieved that she didn't laugh, but kept encouraging me.

Before I had time to lose my nerve, I sent for the information. My palms were sweaty as I opened the long, white envelope when it arrived with the questionnaire. After I had filled it out, I was on the verge of getting cold feet about returning it, but Sharon gave me another boost of encouragement. I wanted to hug her for believing in me!

I made her promise *NEVER, EVER* to tell anyone. I wasn't even going to tell our parents until I absolutely had to. That would be when the first letter arrived, that is if I ever even got one. I was still doubtful, but I was excited, too. I wrote out a check for the correct amount and mailed it with the questionnaire.

I didn't have long to wait until a letter saying I had a computer match with a man in Kentucky arrived. I made up my mind that I wasn't going to write first, no matter how long it took. I would wait for 'him' to write to me, first. Tom's letter arrived after only a short wait.

There were two things I had decided to tell anyone who wrote to me in my first letter. First, I would tell them that I had Muscular Dystrophy and second, I would tell them I am a Seventh-day Adventist. If they didn't like that bit of truthful information, I figured they need not bother to write to me again. Most of them did.

When I told Mom and Dad about my entering Computer Match, Dad's words thrilled my heart, "More power to you, Nancy," he said.

It was August of 1969, and I was almost twenty-five when I was matched with Doug. Everything about him seemed just perfect to me. Maybe now the Lord would bless this friendship and it would mature into a dream come true: marriage. When Doug wrote asking for more information about the fundamental beliefs of my faith, I was jubilant. That's what I wanted; a guy to ask questions because I wasn't going to push my religion on anyone. Without wasting any time, I sent him two books I thought would be helpful.

I was confident that no matter what obstacles came our way concerning religion, we would work them out. As far as my having M.D., he wrote in his second letter, "So what, you're not the only person in the world with a physical problem. I have what's called Addison's disease." I was a wee-bit angry the way he said that, but it also pleased me.

The sun was shining brightly and the foliage was painted in a multitude of colors. The phone began to ring and my heart turned topsy-turvy. Was that Doug calling me because it was my birthday? It was indeed Doug!

For the next hour-and-a-half, he asked an abundance of questions. He had read the two books from cover to cover and had written down questions on paper to ask me. While we talked, every now and then Doug would mention the Addison's disease he had. *"He talks about that so easily as if it's nothing. I've never been able to talk about my Muscular Dystrophy that freely. That's amazing!"* I thought to myself.

Without my realizing it, God was using Doug to help me. Healing in my own heart took place. I began to accept and to be able to talk about Muscular Dystrophy more freely. I had never been able to do that before and I resented even more when others made any comments.

Doug had forgotten that it was my birthday, and I didn't mention it until nearly the end of the phone call. We made plans to meet in Danville, Virginia the next weekend. It wouldn't be far for him to drive from his home in Greenville, South Carolina. Unfortunately, Doug was unable to make it because of illness. Such a disappointment! Before we had a chance to meet, he terminated our relationship because he felt he could not accept my church beliefs.

My heart was sad for nearly a year afterward. In the night, tears soaked my pillow. I was becoming cynical again and doubting the reality of Romans 8:28, "And we know that all things work together for good to them that love God...."

It was hard to get interested in corresponding with others when they wrote to me. I would always reply and after another letter or two from them, nothing. They no doubt could sense that I wasn't interested. It went on that way for a year. Somewhere in the corner of my heart, I had hoped Doug would write and want to pick up where we left off, but that never happened.

Jim and I had been corresponding for several months. We had been matched in January, 1972. After another letter or two in the spring, once more there was nothing. I was caught in an envelope of loneliness and despair. Now where was I to turn; my two years with Computer Dating had expired. In the meantime I continued to keep busy with the Primary Division in Sabbath School.

And I prayed a lot. Or I should say rather, I begged God to work a miracle in my life for once.

Since I did not have an outside job, I wanted something useful to keep my mind off myself. I was petrified to go out looking for a job for fear I would be turned down. It never occurred to me to fight to prove my abilities; I was too short on courage.

In the fall of 1973, I had matured more and dug up some courage that had been stored away somewhere until I needed it. I called the Veterans Administration Hospital in Beckley to see about doing some volunteer work. With butterflies in my stomach, I drove to the hospital for my appointment.

I wasn't sure where to park the car, but I knew I could not step up from a curb onto the sidewalk unless I was holding onto something. It was against hospital policy to park in front. However, that was the only solution to my problem at the moment. There were a few other cars parked in front, anyway. Monkey-see-monkey-do, so I decided not to worry if a ticket was placed on the car while I was inside.

Whenever I would be out somewhere alone, I would ask God, "Please, don't let me fall down." I got out of the car and walked up to the entrance. After pushing the elevator button for the sixth floor, I prayed and wished I could walk standing straight. When I found the right office, I was met by a lovely and friendly woman named Sandy. Her cheerful personality put me at ease and made me feel like I was normal right away. She led me into Mr. Lilly's office as if she had known me all my life.

Mr. Lilly was friendly, but I was still nervous. After a little interview I was afraid he was about to turn me down. After all, most people think if you have a noticeable physical problem, what worthwhile thing can you possibly do?

When I mentioned I typed a little, he decided I could do volunteer work in the library. So, for four or five hours on Mondays and sometimes on Tuesdays, I worked in the library for a year.

Whenever I drove to the parking lot on the days I worked, I always prayed, "Lord, help me find a place to park which isn't too far away." Then, when I got out of the car and started up the walkway, I would say another prayer. "Please, Lord, don't let me fall." It took all the strength I had to hold myself up. If I had to make a sudden turn without holding onto something, I would lose my balance and fall.

Some snow had fallen, but it only remained on the grass as I pulled into a parking space one Monday morning. There, on a bench, a young man was sitting. I kept hoping he would go away as I got out of the car. I was still self conscious of how I walked and stood. People would stare and I hated that! Anyway, he still stayed there reading and I said "good morning" as I walked by him. He glanced up only long enough to return my greeting and went back to what he was reading. He wasn't staring.

Further up the walk, the concrete was broken up a little and I always tried to be cautious when I walked on it. However, this morning I almost lost my balance. In order to keep from falling, I bent myself forward and grabbed my knees. Now I needed to raise up, but I could no longer do it myself because the muscles in my girdle area were too weak. Therefore, I had to have something or someone sturdy to hold onto to pull myself up. *"How am I going to get up, Lord? Please help me."* Then I remembered the young man sitting on the bench a few yards back and called for his help.

Later when I had time to think about the incident, I could see God's hand in placing someone in the right place at the right time to help me in not just one way, but two.

The library had been taken care of by volunteers for a little more than a year because the hospital was short of funds for a full-time paid librarian. It was fun having my own desk to work at. Then, in July of 1974, a full-time librarian was hired. I was a wee-bit jealous of Shelly because I couldn't work at the main desk anymore, but she was a warm and friendly person. Right away she made me feel included. She gave me a special place to do my work and I gained more knowledge on how to be a librarian.

I had been a volunteer at VA for a year when out of the clear, blue sky came a letter from Jim. He apologized for neglectfully not writing. He said he had no real explanation why he stopped writing, but he hoped I would be forgiving. It had been two whole years and I was hesitant about answering it. After waiting a week, I did cautiously answer his letter. No way was I going to let him hurt me again. I suggested if he wanted to continue our friendship he should plan a trip to Beckley soon without much delay. He was signing his letters "Love," which I thought was a bit premature. He said he felt he was falling in love with me. I still signed mine, "Sincerely."

Big January snow flakes had been falling all day. A little while before seven o'clock Saturday night, Jim drove into our driveway. He had come all the way from Lockport, Illinois. I made it a point to meet him standing up so he wouldn't be in for anything unexpected. I had tried to explain M.D. in my letter as best I could. Nervously, I answered the front door.

When we were sitting all alone on the love seat, this six-footer wrapped his arms around me and gave me a kiss. My first kiss. (It's embarrassing to tell how old I was when I received my first kiss). As much as I didn't want to admit it, I could tell the kisses were not genuine. He only kissed me out of pity.

Jim left the next day, Sunday. The snow was getting deeper, which gave him an excellent excuse to leave before noon. A week or ten days later I received a long letter. I was a little uncomfortable. In his next letter, which was his last, the words slapped me in the face cold with hurt, anguish, and humiliation. I didn't want to read the words a second time, but I did. Although I didn't really care for him affectionately, the words hurt cruelly.

"...I was shocked when I saw you...I don't see how you could be a wife, or how you could possibly have sex...."

The more I thought about Jim's letter, the more bitter and angry I became. I knew that I was an attractive young woman who'd just turned thirty, with a zest for life, and a sense of humor.

I *refused* to believe the reason that no man wanted to marry me was because of my disability. However, as angry as I was, I couldn't help but wonder if maybe that was just what every man thought when we met. *"Maybe, just maybe, I am to be single for the rest of my life."*

I gritted my teeth and wrung my hands with the letter still in them. I began to plot how I would take out some revenge on him. I realized my plans might be futile, but at least I would get a little satisfaction out of it.

I decided that my first step would be to write a letter to get my pictures back undamaged. When five or six months passed, I mailed Jim the pictures I had of him.

Oh, how I wanted to rip the wallet size picture into itsy-bitsy pieces, but I didn't. I didn't want to tear up the ones I had taken because I paid for them. After wrapping the three pictures in a blank sheet of paper, I put them in an envelope, addressing it to him. Instead of a return address, I put only "Mrs. JWS," then I mailed it with no stamp. It was my hope that the post office would think I had forgotten to put a stamp on it, deliver it to him and have him pay the postage-due. Also, I especially wanted him to notice the "Mrs." in the upper left-hand corner.

The initials "JWS" were of a friend I was writing to from time to time, although I knew nothing serious would ever come of it. I just wanted Jim to think somebody loved me, and nothing else mattered.

Chapter Eleven

Sharon knew about my frustrations with clothes because I spent a lot of time with her after I graduated from high school. I was no longer able to buy a dress that would fit me and feel right. Sharon, being a clever seamstress, came up with the idea of taking out the slack in the back of my dresses and blouses at the waist. Then she would sew a mock belt across the seam. To know where to take up the slack, I always had to try the outfit on so she could see where my waist would be. It never corresponded with the pattern. Sharon was my mirror.

That eliminated the problem with the back because after I worked on it, it would hang smoothly considering the circumstances. But in front, my ribs always seemed to be poking through everything I wore. My heart ached and I cried inside. I was searching for the right fabric that would work magic and hopefully stop my ribs from showing through.

In the night when I couldn't sleep, a new idea for a creation would dance across my mind. Maybe if I made a dress this way or that way, I thought to myself, maybe it will be a dream come true. Unfortunately, it hardly fulfilled what I had hoped it would when I made my new creation. More tears would flow. Sometimes I ended up giving the dress away.

Sharon was not always around when I was making something new to wear. One day as I was finishing a blouse, I asked mom to be my 'mirror' and pin the back of the blouse in the proper places. She was trying to understand what I needed her to do. I guess I wasn't making myself clear to her.

"Why can't you understand, Mom, what I need done?" Finally in desperation I picked up the box of pins and slammed them vehemently on the kitchen counter and walked off to my room to cry, closing the door behind me.

The devil was trying every angle in the world to destroy me. Now, in my discouraging moments, the old thoughts of suicide would get resurrected. "Oh Lord, please help me. Why do I have to be the one to have all these problems with getting clothes to fit neatly? There is one way to end it all, or is there?" The devil was having a field day with my Christian life. I had accepted having Muscular Dystrophy, but I hated the heartaches it gave me.

In the kitchen, Mom was holding back her own tears while she picked up the scattered pins which had landed mostly on the kitchen carpet. Picking up pins from a carpet is never an easy task!

I was still feeling sorry for myself when Mom came into my room with the box full of pins. She sat down beside me on the bed and cradled me in her arms. Her eyes were moist with tears and her voice quivered as she said, "Honey, if I could trade places with you, I would do it gladly." No parent can bear the sight of a child's suffering and I could never bear Mom's crying because of my hurt. She tried to conceal her tears from me. Now, I consoled her. "I'll be all right Mom, don't cry."

Even though I can accept other people with physical problems better now, I find it difficult to explain Muscular Dystrophy to children and adults who may ask questions. I don't mind their asking. Often times, a simple answer will come to me for their questions when I am just thinking to myself. But when I'm asked a question, I'm at a loss for the words I need to use to make it simple, especially when I'm asked by a child.

Once when I was walking out of the church, a child in the arms of her father pointed and I overheard her say, "What happened to her back?" Quickly the father put his hand over her mouth and whispered something into her ear. The child must not have been satisfied with her father's answer, because the next week the little girl asked her mother the same question. Her mother responded by saying, "She had a boo-boo."

I was so angry with that mother that I wanted to pull her hair out! But then, Christians don't do such things. I asked the Lord to heal my hurt, and decided the best way to settle this little girl's questions was to call the mother later in the week to explain why I am the way I am.

Chapter Twelve

I tried never to doubt God's love for me, but sometimes I felt like He loved and cared for other people more than me. "Lord," I cried many times, "Don't you care about me?" My loneliness would trigger an explosion of tears. As I lay awake crying, the tears would fill my ears and soak my pillow.

I ached inside, a physical ache, because *I was so lonely.* I had nearly a dozen nieces and nephews who were already married and they were *all* younger than I was. Family reunions weren't much fun anymore, because everyone, it seemed, had someone, and I was alone. I kept my feeling to myself, because I didn't want anyone feeling sorry for me.

Why the people who were so strong and healthy seemed to think of us with physical problems as if we did not have the same desires and rights as they did was perplexing and always made me a little angry. "They are so naive," I thought to myself. "They have no humanity or compassion in their blood at all!" One thing was certain; I didn't want their pity.

Some people had suggested that I should marry someone with a physical disability. "So you would have something in common," they said. It puzzled me why they always thought they knew what was 'best' for me and I didn't.

When the gasoline prices started soaring in the seventy's, my mind became a wilted tangle of fear and doubts. To me, it was another obstacle that would keep me a single woman for life. I poured my thoughts and fears into the patient ears of my mother.

"Mom," I said hesitantly, "If these gasoline prices keep going up, I'll never get married."

"Why do you say that, Nancy?"

"Because if I'm ever to meet someone of my own faith, he will have to travel a long distance. He won't want to spend a lot of money for gasoline."

"Honey," she replied, putting her arm around me for closeness and comfort, "When the right one comes along, it won't matter to him how much gasoline costs, because you'll be worth it."

"Why, I hadn't realized that! Oh, Mom, I feel so foolish." Her words of wisdom had lifted my crumbled spirits.

Unknown to me, five hundred miles away in a little corner of the state of Michigan was a gentleman who was as concerned about the price of gasoline as I was. To solve his dilemma, he filled several barrels full of gasoline while the price was low, and stored them around back of where he lived. When it was time to refill the gas tank of his motorcycle, he siphoned it out of one of the barrels.

Motorcycles can go a long way on a tank of gas, so it wasn't being used very fast, and there was a law against storing it this way. He decided he'd better use it faster, so he started filling his mother's car, too.

Chapter Thirteen

Days had evaporated into months and months into years. *"Lord, I'm thirty years old and still single,"* I thought to myself as I settled back to relax in my seat on the plane. I was flying to Memphis, Tennessee to spend several of the winter months with Sharon and her family.

I had quit my job as a volunteer at the VA hospital and someone else was taking care of my Primary Sabbath School class. I had done it for four years and I needed a change.

I had to change planes in Nashville and being handicapped, I was put on the plane first. This time I received an unexpected surprise. In fact, I was privileged. I was given a window seat in the 'first class' section of the plane, which meant I could have free liquor if I wanted it.

When the stewardess asked me if I wanted any liquor I replied, "No, thank you," thinking she had said "literature." My purse was all I wanted to carry so I told her, "I have all I want to carry." My seat-mate mentioned that he never drank his, as he pulled the two small bottles from his coat pocket. He said he always took it home with him since it was free. It was then that I realized the stewardess had said "liquor" and not "literature."

A sneaky grin crossed my face. "Why not?" I thought.

"Stewardess, could I have one of those bottles of liquor?"

"Sure, you can have both it you like."

"No, one will do just fine. I want to have some fun with my minister brother-in-law."

Whenever I fell down when John was around, he would teasingly ask me what I had been drinkin'. So, I decided to wait until I had fallen again, then when John asked me what I had been drinkin', I'd pull the small bottle of liquor from my purse. Later when I presented the little bottle to him, he got one of the silliest smiles on his face and gave me a big hug.

I was visiting with Sharon and John for a while when John first began his ministry. One day, after visiting some of the church members, he came home and told us about his day. Not knowing I had not accepted the M.D. yet, he mentioned that one of his members asked him how his wife hurt her back. (Sharon and I looked so much alike, some people thought we were twins. Some got confused and thought I was Sharon.) I turned white and silent. John noticed he had hit a sensitive spot. He hadn't meant to hurt me. He was always more like a brother to me than an in-law.

One night while I was preparing to go to bed, I fell and sprained my left ankle. For two weeks I couldn't walk at all! This gave me the opportunity to have plenty of time to think: *"So what if I walk funny, at least I'm walking!"*

The weather was getting warmer and I was walking again. There was only a tiny bit of tightness left in my injured foot. Matt wanted to take me for a motorcycle ride out in the cow pasture. He was a real rascal and loved to tease. For nearly an hour we rode. Whenever Matt could, he guided the bike right to the edge of the ravine or to the very edge of the pond full of frogs! That's when I would dig into his ribs.

"Matthew Irving, you're crazy! Don't get so close!" I demanded.

I was the one who was crazy for going out on a motorcycle with a nephew half my age.

He showed me all the nooks and turns, then it happened. The motorcycle stalled and before Matt could put his foot on the ground to hold us up, we started falling over. We landed in some cow dung!

Matt's ego was crushed a little because he failed to keep us from falling over, but we were giggling and laughing just the same.

"Matt, how am I going to get up. We don't have a chair way out here?"

"Don't worry Aunt Nanny, I'll lift you up." (The nickname 'Nanny' came from Matt when he was small.)

We giggled and laughed some more. Fortunately, the dung was dried out.

(My beloved nephew, Matt, was killed in an auto accident September 15, 1979. He was only nineteen.)

During my visit, Sharon came running up to me excitedly. "Nancy! I got something here I think you'll be interested in." Bewildered, and wondering what was coming next as she unfolded the piece of paper in her hand, I waited impatiently for what she would say next.

"Look, I think there's hope for you after all to get married."

We'd had a long talk the week before about how I might be single for the rest of my life since it did appear I was going to always get weaker as time went on. I never told her what Jim had said in his last letter.

"It's something new called 'Adventist Contact' for Seventh-day Adventist singles. Now you can meet someone of your own faith!" she remarked.

We were looking at a 'referral sheet' of someone in the Memphis church who had joined Adventist Contact, and a copy was sent to the minister of that church, which just happened to be John, for him to sign and send back if this individual was a sincere Adventist Christian.

"Here's the address that you can write to for information."

"Now I wonder who is more excited about this, me or you?" I said with a laugh as I walked to the bedroom to get a letter on its way.

Maybe, since these guys were Christians, I would have a better chance of finding someone who would love me for me. I wouldn't have to worry about converting them to my faith since they were already Seventh-day Adventists. I was almost afraid to be hopeful.

Quickly, I sent for the information. When it came, I got a little hesitant. I would have to send in two pictures of myself. One was to be a close-up, which I didn't mind. The other was supposed to be a full length photo, which I did mind. It had been years since I let anyone take any pictures of me standing up. I would only allow them taken of me sitting down.

Another year went by. Finally, I decided to send a picture of me sitting down and hoped it wouldn't be rejected. When a referral sheet was sent to someone, they were sent copies of the pictures along with information about the color of hair, eyes, height, etc.

After a little more than a month of waiting, I received my first three referrals. I waited for the guys to write me first. Two of them wrote and the other didn't. I didn't respond to one I heard from, but I did respond to the other. We corresponded for several months, then he came to visit me. Since he had the summer off because he was a teacher, we saw each other a number of times through the summer. It was never anything but friends. He wanted to continue corresponding, but I didn't. I was afraid to say so for fear he wouldn't like me as a friend anymore and I needed a friend, I thought. He was nine years older than I, with no sense of humor and he was boring. Finally, I got up the nerve to terminate the writing.

1976 was nearly over and the snow was over a foot deep outside. I had no idea which direction my life was going, but one thing was sure; I needed God's help more now than ever. "Lord," I prayed, "If You have marriage in mind for me, please help me to be patient. But if it's Your will for me to stay single for the rest of my life, then show me how to be happy in that role."

In late January of 1977, I was corresponding with a literature evangelist in a mid-western state. He sounded interesting and outgoing. However, two things were bothering me. R.D. had mentioned he had been in an auto accident which caused his back to be injured some. *"What if he had to lift me someday, Lord? Would he be strong enough?"* The other thing that bothered me a little (and I didn't want to admit it), was that the literature evangelists I'd known earned only a small income to live on. Maybe they weren't all poor, but that was the impression I always got.

"O.K. Lord, You have to handle this one. If he should be the one, show me the way. I leave it in Your hands."

Chapter Fourteen

It was a beautiful, sunny day in February, 1977. The snow had finally melted. It had been one of the worst winters in a long time and there were only a few patches of snow here and there. For the first time in nearly three months we could see the ground, even though it was still very wet and soggy from the melted snow.

I decided to clean the kitchen stove. Every now and then, I gazed out of the kitchen window and feasted my eyes on the beautiful sunshine. As I did so, I thought about the dandelions which would be sprinkled all over the lawn in a few weeks with their sunny, yellow flowers. My heart was singing with happiness. Dandelions had always appeared to me as being an ugly flower, but for the first time in my life, I was actually looking forward to seeing them in a few weeks as the weather continued to get warmer. It seemed as though they would bring forth new birth and hope for me, somehow. How little did I know that the day was to be the beginning of a new life for me.

It was just about time for lunch, so I put aside the soapy Brillo pad.

While I ate my lunch, Dad had noticed that the mail had been delivered and had gone to the mail box to get it. When he returned he laid a long, white envelope with the words 'Adventist Contact' on the counter. He had a big smile on his face as he walked away with the rest of the mail. Oh, how he *loved* to tease.

By now, I had decided not to get excited when I received another envelope telling me who I had been matched with. After all, I had joined Adventist Contact a year earlier and I was still single.

As I finished chewing the last bite of food I had in my mouth, I opened the envelope and unfolded the referral sheet. There was a picture of this guy who appeared as though he could stand to lose a few pounds. He was thirty-four years old and he was going to Andrews University in Berrien Springs, MI. Along with the 'vital statistics' was also a list of his interests. 'Foods and nutrition' caught my eye. That gave me the impression that he liked to cook, (I could see that he liked to eat). I didn't mind a man who enjoys cooking, but what I feared was that he might be a man who's apt to tell his wife *how* to cook. And he had red hair. I *hate* red hair. This man sure wasn't what I had been dreaming about. Although he was interested in motorcycles (which gave me the impression he could be outgoing), I just wasn't sure about this one.

Unknown to me, while I was looking at his referral sheet, five-hundred miles away, he was composing a letter to me.

Oh well, I thought, *remember Nancy, you turned everything over to the Lord a few months ago instead of trying to do everything yourself.* It wasn't but a few days later that I received a letter from Edward.

I opened the envelope and began to read the letter.

"Dear Nancy,

Receiving your referral was an especially nice surprise since it came on Valentine's Day!…"

"Humm," I was thinking out loud, "trying to be sentimental, is he?"

Most of my memories of that day have vanished from my mind just as the tiny grains of sand on the seashore become lost in the tides of time, but I do remember noticing his penmanship. It was small, and he pressed hard with his pen as he wrote. I got the impression that he must be quite shy. He signed his letter,

"Lovingly, Ed." I thought that was nice, but it seemed to be a little premature for his first letter to me. Did he sign off like that with every woman he wrote to?

Chapter Fifteen

Spring was in the air. The robins were singing their songs, crocuses had pushed their way through the dark-brown earth, and the yellow forsythia bushes brightened the April days. Dandelions dotted the sunny spots on the landscape.

Even though I wouldn't admit it, I was a little excited about the fact that I was going to meet Ed that night for the first time. Even though we had been corresponding for less than two months, I had a feeling from his letters and a recent phone call that he could be interested in me. He knew that I had M.D., but he hadn't seen me standing up or walking yet. I was trying to play it by ear—I didn't want to be hurt again.

I busied myself in the kitchen preparing a vegetarian lasagna, and baking a chocolate prune cake. I chose these two favorites of mine because I didn't know what he liked yet. As I was chopping the onions, I wondered to myself, "What is Ed really like." He had called for the first time about five days before, and at the time he had no plans to come to West Virginia for a couple more weeks. His voice had confirmed that he was shy, even though he did most of the talking. He filled in the empty spaces between words with a nervous little laugh.

The next evening he called again to ask if it would be O.K. if he came to visit the next week-end, which meant Easter week-end.

"Sure," I replied, "why not?"

At first I wasn't going to make any special dishes because I didn't think this guy sounded very interesting. However, Mom insisted I do it right.

Whenever I was going to meet a man for the first time, I seemed to get real nervous. I even suffered from a loss of appetite and sleepless nights. However, this time I felt at peace. I didn't know it at the time, but now I realize it was God who gave me that peaceful feeling.

Nine o'clock in the evening came and went. *"Where could he be? He should have been here by now."* I was expecting Ed to call and ask directions to my home when he got to Beckley. I figured if he left Berrien Springs by seven or eight o'clock in the morning, he should have arrived in Beckley by now.

When nine-thirty p.m. passed, I decided to call his home to find out just when he had left home, or if I had been stood-up. The phone rang twice and Ed's older brother Robert answered. "This is Nancy," I said, "Could you tell me if Ed is coming, and what time he left so I...."

"Edward is coming, but he didn't leave until eleven this morning," Robert said. "He's not due to get there for a couple more hours yet."

"Wow, why did he leave so late?" I was thinking to myself. It was almost as if Robert could read my thoughts. "Edward had some shopping to do before he left." I thanked him for the information and hung up.

"Well, I'm not being stood-up, he's on his way. But does he always get a late start when he goes on a long trip?" I said to my parents in frustration.

Mom and dad went to bed because Ed would not be arriving until nearly eleven p.m. I thought I would settle back in Dad's reclining chair and do some reading while I was waiting for the phone to ring. As the minutes ticked away, I could hardly keep my eyes open and I had to force them to focus on the book.

Shortly after eleven the phone rang. I hurried to pick it up, expecting to hear a male voice on the other end. I was surprised to hear a female operator instead, asking if I would accept a collect call from Ed Carley.

"Yes," I answered in bewilderment.

Ed said, in his usual soft voice and slow way of speaking, "Hello, I'm afraid I don't know when I will get there. I'm in a town called Williamson, but I don't really know where I am."

"Williamson!" I exclaimed. "How in the world did you get there?" *How could a grown man get himself lost so bad?* I wondered to myself.

"You were to travel south, but not that far south," I said sweetly.

Ed mentioned that his brother Robert had written out a map for him to follow, but somehow he had taken the wrong route and he had become tangled up and lost in Williamson, West Virginia. Some people say, "Don't bat an eye when you're going through Williamson or you might miss it. Obviously, Ed had not.

This was an adventure I hadn't expected. The week-end was unfolding a little oddly for me. I was beginning to wonder if God was planning for it to happen this way for a purpose. God seemed to have more of a sense of humor than I appreciated at the moment. I was tired and I just wanted to go to bed.

I pondered what to tell Ed to do since it was so late. I suggested that he get a motel room and finish his trip to Beckley in the morning. I was getting real sleepy and I had no desire to wait up for him any longer that night.

After we had hung up the phone, I went to bed and slept peacefully until seven a.m. when I was awaken by an alarming thought. I had told Ed to get a motel room in Williamson, but there was one big problem. There had been a terrible flood in that area only a few days earlier, and if there were any motels operating (some of them had flooded out), people who had lost everything were already living in the rooms.

"Now, Lord, what do I do?" I told my parents about what I had done. All I could do now was pray and wait AND WAIT.

Mom and dad decided to go to church, and I was thankful for that. I had been thinking it would be much easier to meet someone I had been corresponding with if it would be just the two of us.

The clock struck ten o'clock. *"I guess I had better get dressed."* I tried to explain about muscular dystrophy the best way I knew how in my letters, but it still was not easy to put everything on paper. I thought that the best way to meet Ed would be if I was standing up. If he didn't like what he saw, I reasoned, he could just turn around and walk back out of the door. (I was praying for a very, very extraordinary man; someone who would love me for me.)

It was ten-thirty. The phone was ringing and I hurried to answer it. It was Ed. I gave him the directions to my home, some twelve hours later than I had expected to originally. More waiting. I went back to my bedroom to one more look at the top part of myself in the mirror, (I hated full-length mirrors). I decided to change into a more comfortable pair of shoes. I was getting a wee-bit nervous. I found myself walking the floor. *"This is crazy!"* But I did want Ed to like me at least a little.

After an endless fifteen or twenty minutes had passed, a yellow Datsun pulled into our driveway. The driver cut too far to the left and was going up my brother's driveway, which was adjacent to ours.

I leaned my head out of the back door and waved as he came to a stop. He saw me and realized that he was at the wrong house. He started to back up to our house, but in his nervousness and excitement he didn't see the log that was lying on the side of Bill's driveway. He backed up on top of it, and got hung-up! He couldn't get his car back off, so he had to leave it there.

The man, whom I knew was Edward Carley, came to the back door to meet me. With his left arm across his chest and waving his index finger, the words to tumble from his lips were, "I got my car hung up on a log out there." That, I could clearly see.

"What?" I asked, not sure I had heard correctly (and yet I knew I had).

He repeated the same thing. It sure wasn't the "Hi, I'm Ed" type of introduction I had expected.

Since it was after eleven a.m., and I knew Ed probably had not had any breakfast, I asked if I could fix him something to eat. He said he would wait because it was so near lunchtime.

We went into the living room to chat. Ed sat down on the couch and I sat on the arm of the couch. (I like to sit higher up sometimes, because it is easier to get up again.)

Ed filled me in on what he had done after he called me the night before. As the story unfolded, it seemed quite amusing. Here is his story:

I got up a little later on Friday morning than I had planned because I had gone to bed quite late on Thursday night. I went to a store to get some things for my long trip, which made me even later in leaving Berrien Springs. I wanted to arrive at Nancy's place early in the evening. It was eleven a.m. when I put my suitcase and lunch for two meals in my Datsun Honeybee. My brother Robert had written out the directions for the routes I should follow and traced his finger on the map to help me further. I asked him to write down the approximate amount of miles between any route changes so I would be prepared to look for the road signs at the right places. He told me it would take about twelve hours to get to Nancy's house.

I was hoping, as I drove out of my driveway on Sunset Drive, that I would be able to make up for lost time on the freeways. Traveling through Niles, Michigan, and South Bend, Indiana, was easy because our family had traveled that way many times since we had moved to Michigan nearly seventeen years earlier.

After I had left South Bend behind, I looked at my directions from time to time to make sure I was following the right route. I was a little confused by the directions though—I wasn't sure if I was supposed to go to a certain town and pick up the next route there, or if I needed to look for the route number as I neared the town. I turned the car around and headed back a few miles, because I thought I had missed the correct place to turn off onto.

I was trying desperately to follow the directions, but I really had no idea where I was. I've always been kind of dumb when it comes to following route signs. When I traveled in the past, someone was always with me to tell me where to turn, so I never paid any attention to where I was going.

The miles flew by. I was wishing I had listened a lot more carefully as Robert was telling me the directions. Even if I had wanted to turn around and go back home, I had no idea how to get there from where I was.

As it turned out, I was traveling along just fine until I came to Cincinnati, Ohio. "Route 52" kept running through my mind as I searched for it. I had no idea whether I was going north, south, east, or west. I didn't even know which way was which. I kept following Route 52, assuming that I was going the correct way.

About dusk, I noticed I was on the Kentucky Blue Grass Parkway. I drove and drove, wondering if I was going the right way. I stopped several times when I could, and asked for directions. Looking at my watch, I decided I should be at Nancy's place in about four or five more hours. I pulled out a sandwich from my lunch bag after asking the blessing for the food and asking God for protection as I traveled, and started eating my supper.

I kept following Route 52. After a long while, I noticed a sign that said "West Virginia state line." Seeing that sign gave me a happy feeling knowing that I was going the right way, or at least maybe I was. It was getting darker and darker and the road was becoming narrower and very curvy. The farther I traveled, the more winding the road became. I was beginning to wonder where out in the sticks does she live? Does she live out here in the middle of no where? I had no idea if I was even going the right way.

I drove on a little further until I saw a group of men in uniforms. I thought they looked like boy scouts, but they were from the National Guard. I didn't know why they were there, or what they were doing. Later, I learned there had been a bad flood in the area several days earlier, and they were there to help the flood victims. I had noticed furniture out on the lawns and a refrigerator here and there, but I didn't understand at the time what was going on.

About ten p.m., I saw a general store in the town of Williamson, West Virginia. I didn't know where in the world I was, and I wasn't having any fun at all! "That's a general store? You gotta be kidding!" I said to myself. I thought about going in to ask directions and make a phone call, but it was closed.

I drove a little way further and came to the State police headquarters. I pulled over and parked my car. It was a little before eleven p.m. when I went inside to ask a policeman how to get to Beckley. He told me to stay on the main highway out there, the way I was going, and said it would take about three or four hours. I asked him again how to get there before I walked out. He looked at me a little funny, I thought. "This is the main highway—you can't be serious?"

I decided I had better call Nancy and let her know I'd be much later. I was supposed to be arriving at her house by now instead of being lost out there in the middle of no where. Since I hadn't brought her phone number with me, I had to call home first to get it.

When I called Nancy (collect), she was rather astonished when I told her I was in Williamson. Since the hour was really late, she told me to get a motel room for the night and finish my trip in the morning.

After returning to my car, I decided I would rather keep on driving and try to get to Beckley. Back on the 'so-called' highway, I tried to follow the directions that had been given to me. The 'main highway' was a narrow two lane road. I couldn't drive more than 25 or 30 miles per hour, and even less in some places. The road was very curvy. Again I wondered, "where in the world in these sticks does she live?!"

As I proceeded to make another turn on the winding road, I couldn't imagine anyone driving much faster in the day-light hours. I had never seen such sharply curved roads before in my life. Winding around another curve and driving ever so cautiously, since I wasn't familiar with the 'highway', I couldn't believe my eyes! Just ahead, a section of about half of the road was gone and I had to drive carefully around it. (Unknown to me, the flood several days earlier had caused that section of the road to be washed out and fall into a deep wooded ravine.)

I still kept wondering if I was following the instructions the policeman gave me. It certainly wasn't the route my brother had written down before I left home. If it had been, I might have wondered if I ever would want to return again. Another Adventist Contact couldn't possibly be this difficult to find.

I kept driving ever so slowly. Apparently, I was traveling further south and didn't need to. By the wee early hours of the morning, I arrived in Bluefield, West Virginia. I stopped again and took out the map to look at it, but I had never really learned how to use one, so I put it away and asked directions from a man I saw. Pointing his finger, he said, "Stay on the main highway here and it will take you to the turnpike entrance, then take 77 north." I thanked him and got back into my car.

Not too many miles later, I got on the turnpike and saw a sign which said "Beckley, 32 miles." In less than an hour, I finally arrived in Beckley—just a little before seven a.m. I was truly bone tired and decided to check into the Ramada Inn for few hours of sleep before meeting Nancy. The motel clerk remarked that I must be tired because I was talking quite slowly.

About ten-thirty a.m., after several hours of rest and a quick shower, I called Nancy and she told me how to get to her home. I wrote down the information she gave me and was hoping I wouldn't embarrass myself any further by getting lost again.

After I had found the correct address, I pulled into the driveway. "So far so good," I told myself. The problem was, I drove over to the left into a driveway which led to a trailer. Nancy had been watching for me and saw that I had gone into the wrong driveway. She poked her head out of the back door. Assuming that the woman I could see was Nancy, I started backing up to get to the right house. As I backed up, I did it again—I mean I goofed! I backed my car up on top of a log I hadn't seen which was on the side of the driveway. I was caught and I couldn't get my car off of it!

When I realized that my car would go no further, I got out and went to meet Nancy. It was after eleven a.m.—twenty-four hours after I left Berrien Springs.

Nancy met me at the door. I *wasn't* prepared at all for what I saw. (I'm not really sure what I did expect.) She had told me she had M.D., but I still wasn't prepared. I was shocked! "After all the trouble I went through and she stands like that," I thought to myself. "I want to leave." I couldn't leave though, because my car was hung on the log, so I decided to make the best of the situation as long as I was already there and then not come back.

Nancy was very pleasant and asked if she could get me anything to eat. Since it was nearly dinner time, I declined and said I would wait. We walked into her living room and sat down to get better acquainted. In just a matter of minutes, I decided I liked this woman very much. Right then and there I knew I wanted her to become my wife. She had such a sparkling and wonderful personality.

Ed sure wasn't giving me the impression that he was the man of my dreams. First, he took twenty-four hours to make the twelve hour trip to my home. He couldn't even read a road map and he had a college education! Next, he got hung on a log in the wrong driveway. "What will he do next?" I wondered.

To those of you who are not familiar with West Virginia, I would like to say that it is not all in the 'sticks' as some people teasingly claim. Some small towns are a little hard to get to, but most places can be reached very easily—especially if one knows how to read a map! West Virginia is full of tall, bumpy trees and lots of beautiful mountains. On a drive, the view is breath-taking. Like the song John Denver wrote, it is "Almost Heaven, West Virginia."

I was not aware of Ed's first impression of me, but I could tell he liked my 'nutty' personality and sense of humor. Not only did his lips smile, but I could see his blue eyes smiling, too. I did want him to like me, but I wasn't sure yet if I wanted him to think of me too seriously.

After a while Mom and Dad came home from church. Dad had a way adding humor to any situation, good or bad. Before he even reached the living room, with laughter in his voice he said, "Ah'huh, I know he's drunk; I know he's drunk! He backed his car over a log and got hung up." (Of course Ed did not drink and Dad knew that.)

After a round of laughter, I introduced Ed to my parents. Then I excused myself so I could change into slacks and help mom with the dinner. As I got up and walked away, I could see Ed's eyes following me. I could tell that he was seeing me and *not* my handicap.

When we sat down to dinner, I noticed that even though Ed was a shy person, he sure did a lot of talking. I thought he would *never* get finished eating. I had already finished and, although Ed wasn't boring, I was getting tired of sitting there. Mom and Dad had excused themselves when they were finished, to leave Ed and me alone to visit.

When we had finished eating, or rather after Ed had finished, Mom and I cleared the table and loaded the dishwasher. As we worked, she asked me what I thought of him. I could see a teasing twinkle in her eyes.

"Now Mom, he's nice, but hold your horses," I said.

She told me that while she and Dad were in the living room waiting for Ed to get through eating, Dad had repeated something Ed had said to him while I was helping Mom prepare the dinner. "It seems that guy has his eyes on you, Nancy, because he told your Dad 'One of the first things Nancy will want me to do is lose weight'." (I hadn't said anything to him about his weight, but apparently another Adventist Contact had, so he was aware of every woman's dream.) I wanted to be nice to Ed even though I thought I had no interest in him other than just being friends.

While Mom and I were in the kitchen, Ed and Dad went out to get his car off the log. They had to lift it up some because of the way it was hung on the log. After that task was completed, Ed and I went for a drive and I showed him the interesting sights. One was the bridge that was being built in Fayetteville, the longest one-arch bridge in the world.

We both talked a lot the rest of the day. We stayed up and talked until two a.m. It rather surprised me that someone who had only a few hours sleep in over thirty-four hours could keep going so long. (Mom told me weeks later it was because he thought you were something special, and the loss of sleep didn't matter.)

The next day, Easter Sunday, I knew that if we went anywhere, it should not be too far, because Ed had told me on the phone when he called to say he was coming that he should leave by one o'clock to get some sleep before going to work on Monday.

For breakfast we had some of Mom's delicious biscuits and country gravy with hot applesauce, which Ed had never had before. I suggested we could go to the Beckley Exhibition Mine at the New River Park and maybe tour the coal mine. I had always wanted to tour it, and now seemed like a perfect opportunity.

As were driving along and talking, I noticed an object in the middle of the road. As we got nearer. I could tell it was a blue and white striped railroad cap. And brand new, too!

I yelled, "Ed, stop!" "Get that cap in the middle of the road!"

How could this be—a brand new railroad cap laying on the road? Later, I began to wonder if maybe God had something to do with its being there. After all, this was our first and perhaps only chance for a spark to develop between us and this simple incident did indeed add a bit of youthful spice to our time together.

The cap fit both of us perfectly. In one way, I wanted Ed to have it, but then I thought if he had it, he would remember me every time he would see it. I truly thought we would only be just friends and I didn't want him to be hurt, so I decided to keep the cap.

When we got to the park, we changed our minds about the tour because I had forgotten my sweater and it would be cold inside the coal mine. I mentioned Grandview State Park, which was at least twenty miles away. Ed was interested in going there.

"But," I said, "It will make you late in leaving for Michigan." He said it didn't matter if he left late.

Before we left the one park to go to the other, Ed asked me if I like Pat Boone's music. "Sure!" I told him what a few of my favorites were, not knowing what he was leading up to.

"I've got them," he said with a big smile as if he could be teasing me.

"What do you mean?" I asked as I wrinkled my brow, thinking maybe he had them at home.

"I've got them with me in the trunk—do you want to hear them?"

"You have got to be kidding," I said.

"No, I have them in the trunk."

"O.K., I would love to hear Pat Boone!"

Ed stopped the car and looked in the trunk for the 8-track tape of Pat Boone, plus a few other tapes.

Here it was Easter Sunday and the first song that came through the speakers was 'April Love'. It didn't dawn on me that it really was April. I was only thinking about how nice it was to be hearing some of my favorites.

We both talked about the kind of Christian home each of us wanted as we listened to the music in the background on the way to Grandview. It seemed to me that no matter what I said, Ed agreed. It was what he wanted, or what he believed in, too. He agreed with me about how children should be raised.

I thought to myself, "What is this guy trying to do?" By now, I knew for sure that he had a great deal of interest in me and we had just met twenty-four hours earlier. I noticed how his blue eyes would follow every where I went. He wasn't watching my walk out of pity. He wasn't staring. Those blue eyes followed me with a smile, as though he were interested in the person I was, and they were not seeing anything else. That gave me a feeling of warmth in my heart for him

When we arrived at the park, still talking and listening to the tapes, I asked Ed if he would like to walk out to the main overlook. I made an excuse about having seen it many times already and said I would wait in the car. The real truth was that the park was crowded and I did not want people staring at me if I walked with him to the overlook. Had there been fewer people, I would have said I would go, too.

Ed said he wouldn't go because he would rather spend the time with me. We spent our time together talking and enjoying the beautiful, sunny day. The Rhododendrons were in bloom and they were, for some reason, especially pretty.

Suddenly I noticed my watch and that the time was flying by. It said thee o'clock, then later on it said four o'clock. I suggested that we had better get going so he could start on his long journey home.

Before we left, Ed said that he wanted for us both to say a prayer, then and there, asking God to direct in our lives according to His will because He knows best and tell Him that we would be willing to follow His leading.

I certainly wanted God to lead in my life. However, I also wanted things my way, and that's what I wanted Him to give me. Another Adventist Contact started corresponding a month before Ed did, and for some reason, I thought that the grass on the other side of the fence looked greener. I was sure, or so I thought, that Ed was not the person I wanted to spend the rest of my life with. After all, I reasoned, he couldn't even do a simple thing like read a road map! I really didn't want to push the point however, because I knew that which ever way God's will worked out in my life, I would be a happy person as long as I lived with His love in my heart.

When we got back to the house, I packed a double lunch for Ed. The trip back to Michigan would take twelve hours—that is if he didn't get lost again. (Dad and I helped him to write out some instructions for the correct routes to take on the way home before we had gone out for a drive that morning.) Since it was getting close to five o'clock, Mom said she was going to fix him something to eat before he left.

"No, Mom!" I whispered, "He takes too long to eat." I wanted to get him on his way. But she insisted on warming up some left-overs for him, so I continued making his lunch. There was no chance of changing her mind.

(I didn't know it at the time, but Mom was trying to make sure she got Ed for a son-in-law. She told me weeks after we had met that when she and Dad saw the referral sheet with Ed's picture on it, she thought to herself, "It sure would be nice if he wrote to Nancy. I wonder if he will or not. He looks so sophisticated. He probably won't write.")

With the railroad cap still on my head, I stood on the back steps leaning on the hand rail for support, while Ed put his things in his car. After that was done, he cornered me in the dining room, because there was one more thing he had to do before leaving to go home.

ADVENTIST CONTACT REFERRAL

It gives ADVENTIST CONTACT a great deal of pleasure to introduce you to NANCY

Consider this an introduction. Why not make an effort to get acquainted? DO IT TODAY!

INTERESTS:

Playing piano

Sewing

Cooking

Reading   (Pictures of covered
Collecting   bridges, grist mills)

NAME   Nancy Coleman   SEX   F

STREET ADDRESS   1426 Maxwell Hill Rd

CITY   Beckley   STATE W. Virginia   ZIP   25801

COUNTRY   USA   OCCUPATION Seamstress

DATE OF BIRTH   Oct   BUSINESS PHONE

HOME PHONE   304-252-3805

HEIGHT   5'5"   HAIR COLOR   Brown   EYE COLOR   Blue

ADVENTIST CONTACT REFERRAL

It gives ADVENTIST CONTACT a great deal of pleasure to introduce you to ED

Consider this an introduction. Why not make an effort to get acquainted? DO IT TODAY!

INTERESTS:

Cars, Motorcycles, Bicycles

Visiting points of interest

Gardening, house plants

Cooking, Baking

Nature walks

NAME ___Edward Allen Carley___ SEX ___M___

STREET ADDRESS ___124 Sunset Dr___

CITY ___Berrien Springs___ STATE ___Michigan___ ZIP ___49103___

COUNTRY ___USA___

DATE OF BIRTH ___April 27,___ OCCUPATION ___Student___

HOME PHONE ___616-471-7037___ BUSINESS PHONE _____

HEIGHT ___5'9"___ HAIR COLOR ___Red___ EYE COLOR ___Blue___

Nancy 5 year old

15 year old, last picture taken standing straight

15 years old, 3" spike heels, one and only pair

Niece Christine, Nephew Harold Jr.,
Nieces Dorcas and Jeanie, Nancy

10 years old, Mrs. Evelyn Fralick the first teacher at
the Beckley Chruch School
My best friend Carol Furrow at my right.

*Nellie, Mom, Dad, Peggy Ann, Sharon, with
Nancy (sitting) July 1972.*

Keith, my favorite brother

On a motor-cycle with nephew Matthew Estrada.

Mom and Dad, Married 63 years
before Dad passed away.

On our Wedding day–October 29, 1977
Beckley, West Virginia

Sabbath School Superintendent at Mentone,
California

Chapter Sixteen

All week after Ed left, I had not received a letter from him and didn't know how his trip home was.

I was sure Ed was different from the others and wanted to be more than just friends with me, so it really puzzled me that I had not received a letter from him. A whirlwind of questions, thoughts, and emotions swirled around in my head. Maybe, when he told his mother more about my Muscular Dystrophy, she had influenced him against pursuing the friendship any further with me. And then, there were the thirty-two other referrals from which he could choose. They were spread out from California to North Carolina. There was even one on his own street in Berrien Springs! Another one was in Niles, which was just ten miles away.

Ed had told me that one of the reasons he chose to write to me first was because one of my interests caught his eye. He liked my picture and I like to collect pictures of grist mills and covered bridges. His childhood roots in the New England states sparked his curiosity, because we both had something in common.

I walked back and forth around the house. Finally, I got up enough nerve to ask Mom if she thought it would be improper for me to call him. She told me no, and to go ahead and call if I wanted to. It surprised me a little to realize I was feeling excited about calling someone whom I thought for sure I had no interest in.

The phone rang only twice before Ed's mother answered it. I wondered what Ed had told her, and what she thought about me. When Ed came to the phone I could tell right away he was delighted I was calling.

When Ed talks to me on the phone, there is something about his voice that makes me not want to say anything. I just want to listen to him. It seemed like he had a Swedish accent, which I found interesting. He told me he was *definitely* interested in our friendship, and hoped in time it would be more.

"Well then, why didn't you write?" I asked.

"You told me to wait a week before writing."

"O-oh, I forgot all about saying that."

Ed wrote a letter that very day and I received it a few days later.

I had suggested to Ed on that first visit before he left that he should meet and perhaps date some of the other Adventist contacts, and he said he would. I wanted him to be sure he knew what he might be getting himself into should he really want to spend the rest of his life with me, because that there were many things I could not do. I told him there wouldn't be any children, not because I couldn't have any, but I didn't want to take a chance on their inheriting M.D.

Three weeks after we met, he was planning a trip to Missouri to meet one of his referrals. At the last minute he called to cancel the trip so he could come to West Virginia, instead.

Once again he put his things into the Datsun. Wanting to arrive at my place at least by seven p.m., he knew he needed to start out no later than seven a.m. With the directions in hand that Dad and I had helped him to write down, he backed out of his driveway two hours late. Figuring he could make up for some of the lost time on the highway, he pressed down on the gas pedal a little harder than he should have. He heard a siren as he was speeding along in the state of Ohio and promptly pulled to the side of the road. He showed the patrolman his driver's license and registration, but the officer still questioned Ed if it was his car.

"Yes," he answered.

"Where are you coming from, and where are you going?" the officer asked.

"I'm on my way to Beckley, West Virginia, to see a girl I was matched with on a computer, and she wants me to arrive before too late tonight."

The patrolman seemed to question whether or not Ed was telling the truth, because he kept looking at the car and license plate, then back at Ed a number of times.

"This is your car, huh?"

"Yes," Ed answered him once again.

"This is your car, huh; it really is your car?"

Ed was beginning to wonder what the problem was. The patrolman must have thought his story about going to see a computer date was a phony one. Anyway, he wasn't given a ticket. Back on the road again, Ed noticed the patrolman following him. He didn't follow Ed a short distance like one might think. He followed him for miles and miles, and still more miles. Finally, the patrolman must have concluded that this guy was telling the truth, because he stopped following him.

Ed arrived at my house at a reasonable hour, and he didn't even get lost this time.

About mid-morning on Sunday, the phone rang. I had an idea who it might be as Mom went to answer it.

"Nancy, it's for you," she said in a mysterious voice.

I had been expecting the call, but was hoping it wouldn't come until after Ed left for home. As I got up from the dining room table to go to the phone, I whispered in Mom's ear, "Please keep Ed in the dining room."

The male voice on the other end of the line was another referral who had started corresponding with me a month before I received Ed's referral and first letter. I tried to sound normal as I talked, but there were "ho-hums." I had a notion that maybe he might be the right one for me, but I wanted God to do the choosing. I was afraid I would make a blunder in my choice with two men in my life at one time.

"Lord," I said, "I only wanted one man—*not two!*"

Before I had finished talking, Ed wandered into the living room. I knew it would be best to try to hang up as soon as possible. The problem was trying to do it without either of them knowing what was going on.

As I hung up, Ed was standing there with a questioning look on his face and he acted a little hurt. He asked who it was that I was talking to.

My mind was so mixed up. Things were moving too fast, I thought. He cradled me in his arms and promised to be patient. When he left to go back home later that day I could see the concern in his eyes about whether he would get to see me again. I guess the weather matched our spirits. The sky was grey, and rain was falling.

I wondered if I saw tears in his eyes as I watched him pull out of the driveway from the living room window.

Ed had accepted me as I was, but sometimes I had a hard time accepting him because he was overweight. He was a handsome man though, with a head full of thick, red, curly hair. However, the way he had his hair styled could be improved. I thought and thought about ways his hair could be styled to be more attractive. Then one evening when I was watching "Lawrence Welk" on TV, it came to me as Guy and Ralna were singing.

Guy's hair is thick and curly like Ed's. "When Ed comes again, I'll suggest to him that he get his hair cut the same length all over, and blow-dry it with no part in it," I thought to myself.

Needless to say, Ed followed up on my suggestion, and when he came to see me again, he was even more handsome than ever. This guy was growing on me.

Chapter Seventeen

As spring rolled into summer, Ed and I continued to correspond and he would make the trip to Beckley every two or three weeks. After his first trip he planned to leave by seven or eight o'clock in the morning so he wouldn't arrive too late in the evening. After the second trip, his skill to read a road map improved to the point that he didn't have to do any back-tracking, or ask for directions. He could make the trip blindfolded! (That is, if he had to.)

I had often wished that God would speak to me in an audible voice the way He did to the patriarchs and prophets in Bible times. Then I would know which of the two computer referrals He had chosen for me rather than waiting and waiting for Him to remove the mountain of indecision in my mind.

In the meantime, I received another referral, and he started writing. He was ten years older than I, and a divorcee, which made me a little uncomfortable about him.

Ed was in love with me, and loved me for myself. When he held me in his arms, I felt cherished and loved. No man had ever shown me this much love before. There was no pity from Ed. I watched him transform into a different human being during the first twenty-four hours we were together. It was hard for me to believe that anyone could care as much for someone as he did me. His blue eyes followed me and he had a gentle smile on his lips. The way Ed cared for me should have answered my question who God had chosen for me, but I was too blind to see it yet.

All I could do was let time and circumstances take care of the matter. Before long, there was no question about it. Ed was the one God had led into my life to share in a life together. He was strong, and could lift and carry me if I needed that someday. In fun one day, he did just that! It was a very sentimental moment.

On one of Ed's visits, when he was getting ready to travel back to Michigan, he had gone back into the house to say good-bye to my parents while I stayed outside on the patio. They knew how much Ed cared for their daughter. "Ed," Dad said cautiously, "There are lots of things Nancy can't do, and someday she may need to use a wheelchair."

"It doesn't bother me that she can't do some things and may need a wheelchair someday. I'll have nothing else to do but take care of her," Ed told them.

Ed had wanted to propose ever since his third trip to see me, but knowing I wasn't ready to give him the answer he wanted, he waited patiently. (Mom had said, "That guy has the patience of Job!") Ed also wanted me to meet his family and waited patiently for the time I would go. The Lord had removed the mountain and we decided that the first week-end in August would be a good time to meet his family.

He came to Beckley on a Sunday to take me back with him for a week. That night when we were alone, Ed popped the question. He asked me to become his wife. I gave him the answer he wanted. Putting my arms around his neck and smiling, I replied, "Yes, I'll marry you!" With his placing a gentle kiss on my lips, it was sealed.

"I love you!" he whispered quietly.

"I love you, too!" I whispered back. After a few silent minutes, I said, "Hey, I'm getting married; it's unbelievable! I'm a little scared, too!"

Ed felt that everything was just right. He was so calm and relaxed. That calmness soon rubbed off on me. "Marriage is a lifetime commitment, and ours will be special," he said, smiling. I agreed.

Ed was all excited and pleased the next morning to be taking his fiancee to Michigan for a week, but first we had to tell Mom and Dad we were engaged (not that it would be any surprise to them.) And, of course, Mom was on cloud nine because she was getting a future son-in-law she wanted!

Nothing could dampen Ed's spirits as we traveled to Michigan, not even my complaining about how hot it was. To make matters worse, the new bridge at Point Pleasant was closed because some cracks had been discovered. They were taking extra precautions to avoid a repeat of the disaster that claimed the lives of a number of people when the bridge a few miles up the river collapsed nearly ten years earlier. That meant we had to travel more than fifteen miles up on the West Virginia side of the river, across to Pomeroy, then drive those same fifteen miles back again on the Ohio Side of the river. An hour extra out of our way in the August heat! I was wishing I had worn knee caper pants rather than my pretty yellow pant-suit.

We talked a lot about our wedding as we traveled. Ed suggested we go a Justice of the Peace to get married. He thought that would be rather simple and with no fan-fare.

"No way!" I said. "I have always wanted a church wedding. And besides, all my family and friends are counting on seeing me get married and they would be disappointed if i didn't have a church wedding."

We decided that maybe Thanksgiving would be an ideal time to get married. I knew that if we didn't have the wedding before freezing weather, Ed would be traveling to West Virginia on the bad roads. I was thinking ahead, "What if he should have an accident? I would never forgive myself."

As the miles rolled behind us, Ed would tease (he loves to do that). And, of course, he would tell me more about his family. I wasn't nervous about meeting them until we drove into his driveway.

Ed's mother (better known to her four sons as "Ma"), even though she knew I had Muscular Dystrophy, never tried to influence Ed against becoming interested in me, except once when she heard a doctor say people with M.D. end up totally helpless. Ed explained that my type was different and, seeing Ed had changed after his first visit to see me, she never again said anything more. Ed's personality had changed, and she could see he was happy.

I was getting cold feet. "Let's go back to West Virginia. What if they don't like me?" I said as we drove into the driveway.

"They will love you!" he said trying to reassure me.

He ran into the house to announce our arrival, then returned to the car for me. When Ed led me in, the living room was still deserted. The drapes were open, but I hadn't seen anyone while I was still in the car, either. Ed went to look for his mother while I stood by the piano near the front door. I planned to be standing when I met her. I needed her approval.

After we met, Ed told her we were engaged. I watched very closely to see how she was going to react to the news. With a big smile on her face she gave us both a hug of congratulations. "She likes me!" I was so relieved!

I reached for the nearest seat, which happened to be the piano bench. It was higher than a chair and that was nice. It felt good to be sitting again. (When I'm standing for any length of time, my back starts hurting. Even though I've become used to pain because I've suffered with it almost every day of life since I was nine, finding a measure of relief is always a blessing.)

On Sabbath afternoon Ed wanted to take me on a tour of the Andrews University campus. Walking would be too tiring for me and I did not own a wheelchair. (And if I did I would have been too stubborn to use it, so I thought.) I wondered to myself, "What does he have in mind?" He had been a full and part-time student at Andrews a number of years, and worked on the grounds. He proposed that, since he owned a small car, he would drive it on the sidewalks all over the campus!

I opened my mouth in disbelief. "On the sidewalks, you've got to be kidding?" But no, he wasn't, so off we went. Down this sidewalk and that sidewalk—all around the campus. The Datsun just fit on the wide walkways.

Fortunately, because it was Saturday and summer time as well, there were not very many students out walking on them. The few that were around were either walking or resting on the lawn.

"What if you get a ticket for doing this?" I asked.

"I'm not worried about that, and even if they do stop me, I would explain the situation and that you are a special person, and they would understand."

"Well, that's nice to know." I wondered if anyone else had been treated like such royalty.

Ed pointed out the different buildings and made me feel like a very special person. No other man had ever made me feel that way.

When he pointed out the gym, I remembered something that happened there nearly fifteen years before.

I was just out of high school and had come to Berrien Springs to spend some time with Sharon and John that fall. On a Saturday night, we went to the gym to see a film and the rain was coming down hard. I was holding onto John's arm from the car to the gym. When we got near the door of the gym, somehow my right shoe flew off my foot into the darkness. I wondered how I'd find it and was so embarrassed as I mentioned to John that I had lost it. Just then, I heard a lady say, "Did someone lose a shoe?"

Laughing, I said, "I did, thanks!"

At that moment, Ed and I were less than a mile apart and didn't know it. It was almost fifteen years later when we did meet through a computer.

Fortunately, we weren't scolded or given a ticket for being on the sidewalk.

The week flew by so fast that Ed wanted me to stay a second week, but I didn't feel that I should.

What Ed had told his family about me just before I met them I never knew until six years later when his brother Walter called me on the phone.

"You won't believe this, but I'm going to tell you what Edward said about you just before we met you," Walter said as he laughed into the phone. "In fact, I don't know what you'll think of us after I tell you." He said, "When you meet Nancy you'll be shocked! But after a little bit it won't even matter that she has Muscular Dystrophy. And you know what?", Walter went on to say, "Edward was right! It didn't matter. I'm just tickled pink he married you!"

Chapter Eighteen

When Ed brought me home after a week in Michigan, I was depressed. Something was tormenting me. I knew the truth, but I didn't want to admit it even to myself. For nearly a year already I had feared I was getting weaker. The M.D. wasn't stabilizing the way I had hoped it would. My muscles weakened so slowly that I hardly noticed it until one day I would attempt to do something I had done a year or two before only to discover I could no longer do it, or it would be harder to accomplish. It was agonizing!

"Please, Lord, don't let me get any weaker," I prayed. "Not now, I'm getting married." There was a great deal of concern in Ed's eyes as he held me close. Very tenderly he assured me, "No matter what happens, I love you, and I want you to be my wife."

"I love you, too. But what if I can't walk someday?"

"Precious, it won't matter to me if you can't walk, I'll still love you, and I want to be the one who takes care of you."

Ed left the next morning to go home. In the meantime, I began to feel better and rested, and I started feeling more excited about the wedding, too. Mom thought that Thanksgiving was too far off. She said she didn't believe in long engagements, so I thought maybe I should choose a closer date. However, first I needed to check with John and Sharon to find out when John could get away from his pastoral duties in Memphis. We decided on October 29.

When Ed returned at the end of two weeks with his mother, he told me about the cute little apartment he had found. "And it's on the ground level with no steps!"

"Are you going to move in and live there?" I asked him.

"No, I'll wait until we're married, and then I'll move in. I don't want to live there alone. By the way, I'm sure glad you changed the wedding date. I can hardly wait until you're mine!"

"Is that so-o-o!"

Ed had taken some pictures of the apartment and brought them along so he could show me what it looked like. It was indeed small, but it looked cozy. We were glad it was furnished even though I was planning to have my bedroom furniture moved there. After seeing the kitchen chairs, I decided they could stand a new look.

"Honey, when you come back in two weeks, why don't you bring the backs and seats from the kitchen chairs with you. They look like they will come off easily, and we'll get some new oil-cloth to cover them."

When Ed returned in two weeks, he came on Thursday instead of the usual Friday arrival day, because we planned to get our blood test and apply for our marriage license on Friday. After we had taken care of those things in the morning, we went to Murphy's in the afternoon to look for some oil-cloth to cover the chairs.

Just as we stepped into the open double doors at Murphy's, I fell down! *Of all the times to fall.* (I had been noticing for the last couple of years it didn't seem like it was as often now.)

Ed had only seen me fall once since we first met, but he knew to expect it. Even so, it came as a surprise and he was taking a little too long figuring out how to help me up as the people walked by.

When he stooped down to help me, out of blushing anger and with gritted teeth, I whispered into his ear, "If you're going to marry me, you had better learn how to get me up fast! Get behind me and put your arms under mine and lift! Now hurry up!"

We found some pretty oil-cloth to cover the chairs, and using some foam Ed brought with him, we padded and covered the seats and backs Saturday night.

Before Ed left for Michigan, he surprised me with a four-pound box of chocolates for my birthday, which I would be celebrating before his next trip to see me. I had *never* received a box of chocolates from anyone other than a member of my own family.

Even though the wedding was only two short months away, I wasn't too worried about being ready because I wanted it to be simple, yet attractive. I sat down to start making plans. For years I had been planning my wedding day, and was only waiting for 'Mr. Right' to come along and sweep me off my feet. But now, I couldn't remember all those ideas I had filed away in memory. Maybe I should have written them down. I remembered clipping pictures out of a magazine, but I felt they were outdated. Times and things had changed.

The biggest problem for me to solve was my wedding dress. For this one special occasion, deep in the recesses of my heart and soul, I wished that I could be standing up straight with no altering (or tears) to suffer. In reality, I knew that was not to be so. I am the way I am and it can't be changed. I prayed for strength to endure the problems and trials that would be mine. My conversations with God were unceasing.

With a prayer on my lips, I went shopping for that special material with which to make my dress. It couldn't be too heavy or even too light. It had to have the 'just right' body to the fabric, or else it wouldn't hang right for me. I had found some material a few days earlier, but I wasn't quite satisfied with it. I parked the car, and Mom and I walked into the fabric shop. I wandered around, and hoped, and prayed for some pretty white knit. I walked from row to row of fabrics, my back hurting all the time. There it was! Even the price had been marked down.

"Mom, look; what do you think?" I asked with a smile. "And look, here's some green just like it to make your dress."

Mom picked up both bolts of fabric and carried them to the counter. (I could no longer carry anything in my arms.) After we had paid for it, I went home pleased and amazed. The material for my wedding dress cost only twelve dollars! It was really wonderful how God was working out each problem as it came along.

I created my own dress style from several patterns I had. I liked the sleeves from one pattern, the long skirt from another, the top and back from another one. It wasn't unusual for me to do that, as I had created many of my dresses that way. It would have been just super to go out and buy a wedding dress, but I knew that wouldn't work because I had to alter everything I made. I had not been able to buy a dress from a store for over ten years. I had made all of the dresses and blouses that I wore.

After I sewed the dress together and knew it was time to try it on, I prayed. Oh, how I prayed. The Lord knew my heart's desires, and He gave me an extra dose of courage when I put it on so I would not plunge into a deep depression the way I did sometimes when I was making an outfit. While I held onto the bed post for balance, Mom pinned the hem in place. My ribs still showed, but I knew I had done my best. And what was it that Sharon once said when I complained about my ribs showing? "Sweetie, they are protecting your heart and lungs."

The dress was finished in record time. It was another way in which God was telling me that He approved, and was blessing this forthcoming wedding.

In the meantime, Ed was in Michigan trying to find a green suit. I had chosen yellow and green for my colors, and I wanted Ed to wear green. There were plenty of suits which he had tried on that fit him, but it was difficult to find a green one. His search led him to nearly thirty stores in the Benton Harbor, Saint Joseph, and South Bend area. He was trying to lose some weight, too, but he wasn't working all that hard at it. Had I known the problems he was having, I would have suggested another color.

I suppose most men would have complained, or would have given up, but not Ed. He kept searching. He thought if he had to, he would piece together a suit from K-Mart!

Finally, he went to a store in Niles just ten miles from his home to see what they had. It was only five days before the wedding. They didn't have a green suit either—at least not in his size.

However, they said they could order one from Chicago, and it should arrive in two days.

When Ed called me that night, he seemed so calm.

"Are you sure it will arrive by Wednesday?" I asked calmly since he was so calm about the whole thing.

He had no way of knowing for sure if the suit would arrive on Wednesday so he could leave for Beckley early on Thursday morning. (It was to be his twelfth trip to West Virginia.) Nonetheless, the suit *did* come on time, and he never tried it on until Thursday night after he had arrived. Fortunately, the suit fit him perfectly, and all I had to do was to hem the legs since that couldn't be done before he left Michigan. God started performing *this wedding* on Valentine's Day.

Chapter Nineteen

Sabbath morning, I awakened early and the sun was shining through my red draperies. *This is my wedding day!* Happy thoughts flooded my mind. *Well, Nancy, this is the big day you have longed for. No more tears of loneliness to SOAK YOUR PILLOW. "Thank you, Lord, for sending the sunshine today. I don't think I could stand it too well if it were cloudy." I wonder what Ed is thinking right now?*

It seemed like God had everything in control. More happy thoughts flowed through my mind as I lay in my bed, listening to the hustle and bustle of the rest of my family in the dining room preparing breakfast and getting ready for church.

In less than twelve hours, I would have a new title to my name. I looked around my cozy bedroom. Dad and Mom had paneled the room with some money I had saved, a friend had done the ceiling, and I had bought new carpet. Many of my things were already in Michigan waiting for Ed and I to start our new life together. My brother, Harold, would move my bedroom furniture for me.

I rose up onto my knees at the corner of the bed to open the draperies to let the sun shine in unhindered. Oh, how it lifted my spirits even more! I chuckled as I remembered the first date Ed and I had some months ago, and how I thought I 'knew' that this was a man I *didn't* plan to spent the rest of my life with!

"Lord, it's a good thing we put our lives in Your hands."

I decided that was enough reminiscing. It was time to get dressed for church. Things were a little quieter in the next room now which meant most of them had left for church, and I'd have the only bathroom to myself without someone pounding on the door for me to hurry up.

Before I got up, Sharon poked her head in the door and said, "Good-morning Merry Sunshine!"

I wondered when would be the next time I would hear her say that again. It's a wee-bit sad to get married. Many things would change, and I wouldn't get to go visit Sharon as often or stay with her for months at a time, but we had lots of memories together. I was surely going to miss Teresa, Angela, and Matt, too. They were like my own children, and were the only children I knew I would get to 'mother'.

"It's hard for her to see her baby sister getting married, I'm sure. We were so close."

While I was getting dressed, Mom came into my room and asked if it would be okay if she rode to church with Ed and I. I told her "Sure." Since I hadn't had a chance to tell her the details about the wedding, I thought I would do that now. It was our time alone. We had shared a lot of 'talk times' together, Mom and I.

"Mom, when Dad walks with me down the aisle I'll be holding his right arm rather than his left, because it's more comfortable for me. Just after I reach up and give Daddy a kiss, you come around in front of him and let me give you a kiss, 'good-bye'.

She smiled. "Are you trying to get me started crying?" she asked with a broken voice.

Mom had said many times she doesn't cry at weddings, because she is happy for the couple. "I didn't cry when Peggy Ann and Sharon got married, and I don't think I'll cry at your wedding, either, because I'll be very happy for you!"

Mom had told me several months before, "You know honey, I'm very happy you are going to marry Ed. I have been praying that the Lord would allow me to live long enough to see you happily married. I know how lonely you've been and how you hurt."

I knew my wedding was a little more special to Mom and Dad, as well as the rest of the family. Somehow, I couldn't picture them without a few tears.

After church, all the family members of both our families joined together at the house for a pot-luck dinner. It was such a beautiful autumn day, and was unusually warm for this time of the year.

Keith and Joy arrived after dinner; this wedding wouldn't be right without my youngest brother there. As I introduced Ed to Keith I wondered, *"What does he think of Ed since they haven't met until this moment. Come to think of it, I guess most of the family hadn't met him until this week-end."*

The evening air was still warm as I rode with mom and dad one last time to the church I had worshiped in since I was five years old.

I was seated in the library waiting for my turn to enter the sanctuary. Sharon helped me with my veil. In a calm voice, and as a matter of fact, she told me that Ed got lost on his way to the church.

"Lost!" I said in an excited voice, "What do you mean, lost? How... How could he get lost on our wedding day? I showed him how to get from the motel to the church just so he wouldn't get lost or be late."

"He got lost on his way here, but don't worry," she reassured me, "He's here now."

"Why didn't you say so in the first place, instead of alarming me?"

In my last private moments of being single, I sent a prayer Heavenward, asking God to help me to be a loving Christian wife to Ed. I was quite calm and had been all day. It surprised me in some ways, but I knew everything was falling into place because God wanted it that way for us.

I knew that weddings hardly ever start on time the way they are supposed to, so I didn't expect mine to be any different. However, this wedding was being directed from Heaven. Everything was coming off on time as planned. It was time for the candle lighting ceremony and Ed's brother, Walter, and my nephew, Matthew, were the ones who had been selected to light them.

Since Walter had arrived from Michigan so late and had missed the rehearsal, he was at a loss. He had never even seen the church before the wedding. Fortunately, he had Matthew to help him along.

Matthew went up the left aisle, lighting the candles on each window sill, and Walter went up the right aisle. When all the candles in the windows were lit, Walter started walking back to the rear of the church, thinking he was done. About half way to the back, he glanced to the other side and saw that Matthew was at the front of the church lighting some candles. Walter turned around and went back to the front of the church to light the ones on his side. As soon as those candles were lit, he started down the center aisle. He had only walked about two or three pews back when someone stopped him saying there were more candles to light. Once again, he turned around and went back to the front to light more candles. This time, however, Walter wasn't about to walk down the aisle until they were all lit. Matthew kindly pointed out one more candle that he had missed, then they both went down the center aisle together. The smiles on the faces in the congregation told him that they understood.

As soon as they got to the rear of the sanctuary, the lights were dimmed and the wedding march began to play.

I had one big mountain of concern. I didn't want to fall down while I was walking down the aisle in my wedding. I asked the Lord, *"Please* give me strength so I won't fall down on my wedding day!"

Unknown to me, at the same time, in a little room where Ed, John and Roy (Ed's youngest brother and best man) were conversing after John had prayed, Ed asked him what he should do if I fell while I was walking down the aisle.

"Go pick her up and set her on the seat as though nothing unusual happened," John said with a smile.

I knew standing during the ceremony would make me very tired and cause my back to become very painful. I wanted these special, sweet moments in my life to be as blissful and painless as possible, so I arranged for us to sit down during the ceremony facing the audience, which delighted everyone.

For nearly fifteen years, Dad was my support whenever I had to walk in places where I might have fallen without it, or up steps where there was no handrail for me to hold onto. During the last ten years though, he suffered with rheumatoid arthritis which caused him a great amount of pain. Still, he was always there to help me when I needed it.

The wedding march was about ready to be played on the organ. I had gotten a glimpse of my handsome groom. I had to take one more step up into the sanctuary and was trying to balance myself as I took a step forward, but then dad took a step, and I had to take another step to get the balance I wanted before walking down the aisle. *"Dad, stand still! The wedding march hasn't started yet,"* I wanted to whisper, but I didn't. I was expecting Dad to read my mind so I didn't say anything. I had to stand off-balance in order to keep him from walking another step.

Teresa and Angela, Sharon's two girls, were junior brides maids, and Sharon was my matron of honor. All three were dressed in yellow. After Sharon reached the front of the sanctuary, it was my turn. Everyone rose to their feet.

"Lord, please don't let me fall," I breathed one last time. As I walked along, from time to time, I lightly put my right hand on the end of a pew for support. When we reached the front, I gave Dad a kiss, and Mom came over to let me kiss her. In the candle light, I could see that her eyes were glazed over with tears.

"Who giveth this woman to marry this man?" John asked.

"Her...mother and...I."

Dad's voice was broken. Just as he finished speaking, Ed moved over to take my left arm. Dad, being cautious, wasn't letting go very easy for fear I might fall. I was having a hard time slipping my bridal bouquet of two yellow rose buds through his arm, and they bent backward when I changed my hold on his arm to Ed's.

Ed and I walked forward a few more steps and turned around to be seated facing all our relatives and friends. I smiled as I thought about the little 'surprise' I had planned for everyone at the end of the ceremony.

A new season had begun. Autumn was painted in beautiful scarlet and gold. Also, a new life was about to begin for us. We would no longer be single and lonely individuals. Our lives were about to become one.

"Ladies and gentlemen, may I present to you, Mr. and Mrs. Edward Allen Carley." The lights came on and Ed rose to his feet. The organ was playing as he came over to my right side. What is he going to do, many wondered? As though he did it every day, Ed swept me up in his arms and carried me down the aisle. A thrill of excitement rippled through the sanctuary, and then everyone started applauding! There were hardly any dry eyes left when the groom picked up his new bride in his arms.

At the reception Uncle Jack remarked, "Ed's picking Nancy up was the frosting on the cake!"

Chapter Twenty

"Nancy Carol," (Keith is the only one who ever called me by my full name). "You and Ed get in the car, and we'll turn it around for you."

"WHAT!?"

"Get in the car," Keith repeated with a suspicious grin on his face that said, "Do-as-I-say-and-don't-ask-questions." We were leaving the reception, the yellow Datsun still covered with lots of colorful ribbons and bows, and tin-cans trailing behind—thanks to Karel. We could hardly see out of the windows for all the ribbons and white shoe polish!

"Okay, are you ready?" I heard someone ask. Then, in chorus, "One, two, three!" The car was being turned around by my three brothers, Roy and Walter. After several lifts, we were pointed down the driveway.

"Now you can go," Keith said. "Oh, Ed, it sure was a whole lot lighter to lift before you got in." I could tell by Keith's teasing that he approved of Ed and it pleased me. He had not met Ed until only a few hours before the wedding.

·―――――――――――――――――·

I chuckle to myself as I remember how Keith and I got along while we were growing up. He was six years older, and we got along like cats and dogs! But our love for each other was very strong. Keith had his very own guitar, and oftentimes I would hear him playing "The Wildwood Flower."

One day his guitar was leaning up against the maroon couch in the living room, and he was nowhere in sight. I knew he would be gone for quite a while as I walked over and fingered the strings. Picking it up, I decided to have some fun and play it while he was gone. I reasoned to myself that my big brother didn't really know all that much more about music than I did. *"He can't possibly know anything about tuning this guitar, and if I put it back where he had it when I finish playing it, he'll never know."*

Boy, was I ever wrong! When Keith came home later that day, he went into the living room to play his guitar. In a little while, he went storming through the house, yelling at Sharon. "Sharon Louise, have you been messin' with my guitar?" Being only eight years old, I knew I wasn't about to confess my guilt. My teenage brother had a bit of a temper, so I thought I would let Sharon take the blame. She told him that she hadn't touched his guitar.

"Now I got to go to the store and get new guitar strings. I can't get it tuned right," he said as he stormed out the back door. I knew I couldn't out run my big brother, so I stayed hidden. I was beginning to think he knew more about music than I thought he did. After that, I would never touch his guitar.

One time I found a four-month-old grey kitten out in the corn field. I was shocked several days later when I saw kitten, because his beautiful grey fur was saturated with a sticky, oil-like stuff.

Keith had sprayed ant spray all over the kitten. The spray can was the old-fashioned type with a can that you could fill with ant spray, or the like, and had a long handle with a hand pump built into it.

Sharon and I took the kitten into the bathroom and put it in the tub. We tried everything we could think of to get the ant spray out, but nothing worked, not even A-Jax.

Oftentimes when Keith came home for a visit, he would tease me about the time I "fithed" his pocket watch with Daddy's hammer when I was a small child.

._____.

There wasn't going to be any honeymoon, because Ed had to get back to his classes at Andrews to finish his studies which would be completed in March. I was looking forward to seeing my husband wearing a cap and gown at graduation time in June.

It was raining when we arrived in Michigan at our first little home together on Monday. Ed ran to unlock the door, then he hurried back to the car and we walked together to the door. He was looking forward to carrying me over the threshold.

Before we were married, Ed was the proud owner of a brand-new Honda Gold Wing 1000 motorcycle, and it was all paid for, too. However, after our third date, he decided he wanted to sell it so he would have some money saved up. He had marriage on his mind. He knew he wanted to marry me, but I wasn't sure of my feelings just yet and asked him not to sell it. When he came to see me the fourth time, the motorcycle had been sold. I felt a little sick.

On the first Sunday after we had been married for a week, Ed announced that he wanted to borrow the motorcycle from the new owner and take me for one long ride. He knew he would be able to borrow the motorcycle for a while, and told me to be sure and dress quite warm, because "the wind will get quite cold when we get going real fast."

The sun was shining and it was warm for November, so I couldn't see wearing a winter coat. I thought I should be warm enough wearing a long sleeved knit tunic and my big white, warm sweater. After he lifted me on, he put a helmet on my head. *"What a life, this is fun,"* I thought as I wrapped my arms around MY HUSBAND. I was having the thrill of my life. "It doesn't seem too cold at all," I told Ed.

"Wait until we get on Lemon Creek Road, and we'll go faster." As far as I was concerned, we were going fast enough already. Soon the wind was whipping in my face as Ed speeded up to sixty or so miles per hour. When I would try to say something to Ed the wind would blow the words right back into my mouth. I was glad I wasn't being treated like a frail person by the man who loved me dearly. I was beginning to feel the cold air as it penetrated through my two layers of long sleeves. A winter coat would have been better after all, but I didn't want to tell Ed that. I was afraid he might say, "I-told-you-so."

Every now and then, Ed would slow down and tell me about this place or that place. The sun was slipping away beyond the horizon, and it was beginning to get colder. To top it off, it started raining! Ed raced us along to get away from it, if that would be possible, and he was able to do it because it was only scattered showers. My feet and lower legs were becoming a little numb by the time we arrived back at our apartment, and I was having a problem with circulation making it difficult to walk. After I had walked around for a little while, I was back to normal.

There was a lot to do in the weeks and months ahead, and there was never a dull moment with Ed around. It was fun preparing the apartment and making it cozy. And when it came to cooking, I had a great time trying new dishes.

After Thanksgiving, the cold Michigan snow started to fall. Since the weather seemed to be a little milder at Christmas time, we went to West Virginia to spend the holiday with Mom and Dad. I was glad we went, because it was the only Christmas I got to spend with my parents as a married woman in the house I had grown up in.

The little refrigerator in our apartment was barely large enough to hold all of our food. The ice box was really small, so when the snow came after the holidays, we would take our ice-cream and bury it in the snow where it would keep for days without thawing out.

Whenever we went shopping for things we needed, my back would hurt quite badly. It hurt so much that I began to let Ed go alone even though he wanted me to go along with him. We talked about getting a wheelchair, and how to go about getting one. It wasn't much fun not being able to go with him to some places. Someone told us we could get a wheelchair from the Muscular Dystrophy Association.

Ed was late coming home one day, and with the weather outside like it was, I was beginning to worry a little. When he did arrive I asked him where he had been. "I went to Saint Joseph to inquire about how to get a wheelchair for you...." As he filled me in on the details, I noticed how he didn't seem bothered the least bit about my needing a wheelchair. That, and how he went about the whole thing, made me appreciate him even more. Otherwise, I would have been furious with him.

Although I knew I needed a wheelchair sometimes, I still had to get used to the idea slowly. I wanted to walk everywhere possible; it gave me a feeling of independence. And what if I saw the wheelchair as a way out of walking when I should be walking, I reasoned to myself.

On our first trip with the wheelchair, we went to the Sears Tower in Chicago, which is the tallest building in the world. Even though the weather was bitter cold outside, the sun was shining. I dressed like I had seen people in wheelchairs dress—overly dressed. It seemed to me that they always looked sloppy, too. I *did not* want to be like them, so I dressed as neatly as possible, but with only socks on my feet and an afghan over my lap.

When Ed put the wheelchair in the car, I put the afghan over it so it wouldn't be seen because I was embarrassed to even have it near me. I had kept it covered in our apartment too, because I didn't want to see it when I wasn't needing to use it.

By the end of our tour of the Sears Tower, I was getting uncomfortably warm. After that I vowed, "NO WAY am I going to dress this way again! Whenever I need to use the wheelchair, I'm going to dress in the most attractive way possible. I can't walk in flat-heeled shoes, but I can do just fine in the shoes that have two inch wide heels, and they are in style, too." As time went by, I decided I could wear two inch high heels when they came back into style once more. Even though I couldn't walk with them on, there wasn't any reason why I couldn't wear them while I was using the wheelchair. I wouldn't be going anywhere in socks again! No more afghan, either!

"Honey, isn't it time for you to go to your afternoon class?" I asked, seeing Ed was not in any hurry to get going. Slowly, he picked up the book for class, gave me a kiss and went out the door.

The Michigan winter was as bad as it had been the year before, and I was glad Ed wanted to move to a warmer climate when he finished his schooling.

The sky was getting darker. *"Ed should be home soon,"* I thought to myself as I tried to keep busy instead of watching the soap operas on TV to pass the time. *"I hate soaps, I want to quit watching them! Ed's late, I wonder where he is?"* As a new bride, I had a lot to learn about married life.

When Ed came home he made no mention of anything pertaining to the afternoon class. I decided the snow must have delayed him. Several weeks later, I learned more about his afternoon classes, and I nearly exploded. I didn't though, and we talked it over calmly. We were in the middle of getting things settled when the phone rang. It was my niece, Chris. She and her husband lived in Berrien Springs, too. She wanted to know if Ed could help Steve move a refrigerator.

While Ed was gone, I began to wonder if he would always keep things from me, although I hardly thought so. He had taken his text book with him as if he was going to class, only he played 'hooky' instead and drove to see a big pile of snow he had seen on TV news report the night before. My husband, thirty-five years old—I just couldn't believe it!

He was taking a class which required him to get up in front and speak to the students. Because he was so shy, he disliked that idea very much. He knew that he had to take the class in order to graduate, but he put off taking it until the very end. It was the second or third time he had started the course and dropped it, because he just couldn't bring himself to get up in front of the students.

When he returned, we discussed how he was going to graduate. I gained a new insight into my husband's way of thinking, and a better understanding of how he felt inside.

He was able to work it out with his teacher who let him do a research paper instead so he could graduate.

I knew Ed was shy, but not with me. He felt relaxed with me from our very first date together. He shared things with me that I knew he had not told any other human being. He, I could tell, was a sensitive and caring man. On our third date I discovered he *didn't* like buttermilk when I asked him if he wanted a glassful. I had liked buttermilk ever since I was a little girl on the farm in Ohio, and would drink a cool glass of it once in a while.

When I had finished drinking my glass of buttermilk, we walked into the living room. Mom and Dad went elsewhere so we could be alone. While we were seated on the couch together, Ed asked me tactfully, "Would you like a breath mint?"

"No," I replied, blinking my eyes and wondering why he asked.

"Are you sure?"

Now, I knew I didn't have bad breath—then it hit me!

Teasingly, I snuggled up close. "Now I know why you asked me if I wanted a breath mint—you don't like buttermilk kisses, do you?"

He smiled and said, "No."

Chapter Twenty-One

Even though Ed was to graduate with a B.S. degree, he still wanted to work outside in landscaping, but in a warmer climate and for the denomination. Ed was tired of going out in the snow and ice in the winter time, and just to look at the stuff made me fall down.

I typed a resume for him and he got copies made to send to Adventist hospitals. We received a number of job applications, which he filled out and sent back. Some of the places said they had no openings.

It was about the first of March, and Ed still hadn't received any job offers. He needed to have a job by the last of March, because that's when his studies at Andrews would be completed, and he would no longer have a job at the grounds department after that, since he wouldn't be a student any longer.

We prayed about this, and I could see that Ed was getting a little nervous. In the meantime, Hinsdale Sanitarium near Chicago was aware that Ed was looking for a position even though he had not contacted them. *"Could the Lord be calling us there?"* we wondered. We knew it was cold—very cold in Hinsdale. Ed asked me how I felt about it, and I told him the decision was his to make. I had vowed to myself not to interfere.

About a week later, Hinsdale Sanitarium called. I was sick in bed when the phone rang. After Ed answered it, he told me who was on the line. I mumbled under the covers, "It's cold there and

I don't want to move there." Ed told them what I had said, and that we wanted to move someplace where it is warmer.

It was the twentieth of March, and it was a warm, sunny day. The phone started to ring, and I answered it.

"Is Ed Carley there? This is Paul T____calling from Loma Linda University Landscape Department." *Is he going to ask Ed what I think he is going to ask him?* My thoughts raced excitedly. Trying not to sound excited (in vain), I replied, "No, he's at work, but this is his wife. Can I take a message?"

"We're offering Ed a job at the landscape department* here." That was the call we were hoping and praying for; the Lord is so good! I could hardly wait until Ed came home. Not long after the call, I heard the front door open. "You're home early. Guess who called?" I blurted out. Ed told me Paul T____had called him at work and asked if he'd like to come to Loma Linda.

"A-n-d..?" I could hardly wait for him to answer.

"I told him I would take the job and that I would be there ready to start work on the fourteenth of April."

"YIPPEE, CALIFORNIA HERE WE COME!"

Ed had already gone to the local U-Haul rental office and put a deposit on a truck. We had the bedroom set which I had brought from West Virginia when we got married, and lots of boxes of wedding gifts to move. The little datsun wasn't equipped with enough horsepower to pull the size trailer that we needed to haul our belongings. As it turned out, it was cheaper to rent a large truck than it was to rent a smaller one, and the large truck was so big that Ed was able to put the Datsun inside rather than having to tow it behind.

Before leaving for California, we took a quick trip to West Virginia to see my parents, because we didn't know when I'd get to see them again. While we were there, Ed wanted to take me to Williamson, just for old time's sake. He wanted me to see those

---

* *As of December, 1987, Ed is employed by the Loma Linda University Power Plant.*

sharp, curvy roads. I thought we wouldn't be gone for more than two or three hours, so I didn't pack a snack-supper. We left about three o'clock in the afternoon. Using a road map, I acted as the navigator. After what seemed like hours of driving, we came to the very winding road that had brought Ed to my home on his first trip to see me—the road that brought him to my home and eventually into my heart. I looked with amazement at the part of the 'highway' which had fallen into the wooded ravine almost a year earlier. It had not been repaired yet, and I wondered how it even could be repaired from the looks of it.

"Honey, there is no way you could have driven this road in the dark without your guardian angel. He kept you awake and watched over you with very special care," I remarked. Ed agreed.

It had taken three hours to get to Wiliamson, and it was getting dark. With no food in the car, we wondered if we should stop and get some, or could we make it for the three hours it would take us to get back home. Finally, Ed decided to go into a supermarket. When he came back to the car, he said he didn't know what he should get, "So I got these cake-doughnuts." I smiled, "That's okay, I'm hungry for anything." He was wishing he had bought bananas instead, even though they were quite expensive. We asked the Lord's blessing for our food and a safe trip back to Beckley.

We finally drove into my parents driveway at mid-night. It took even longer getting back than we had thought, because it was dark. Dad met us at the door, and said he was really beginning to worry about us. He was about to call the state police when we drove in. We crawled into bed, bone tired.

It was raining when we left Berrien Springs to start the long trip to California. We were looking forward to living in a warmer climate, but it was also a very sad time, because we were leaving our families behind not knowing when we would get to see them again. Ed's mother had wanted to have a farewell supper for us, but it didn't work out so she could. Ed didn't know what to expect of California. He had heard that it didn't rain much except in the winter months. I tried to tell him all I knew, since I had been there several times.

The trip was slow at times, and we ran out of gasoline in the middle of Oklahoma City on Interstate 40. Ed had to walk to a service station. Fortunately, a station was in sight from where we were stopped. I watched him getting smaller and smaller as he walked away. I started to feel grumpy while I sat there waiting, because of the delay, and I was getting hot as I watched the traffic zoom by.

We went through the painted desert and the petrified forest in Arizona. It was a special treat for Ed. He had never seen it, but I had when I was sixteen years old. Afterward, we stopped at a pizza place which was a welcome treat for both of us. The trip was like a mini honeymoon, since we didn't have one when we were married.

When we arrived in California, Peggy and Don let us rent one of their houses until we found an ideal place to locate. In June we moved into a house that fit our needs and had enough land for Ed to plant a garden and some fruit trees.

Since we were over 2,200 miles from Andrews University when it was time for graduation, I was a little disappointed because we couldn't afford to go back. However, Ed was glad we were so far away. If we were still living in Berrien Springs, he would have had to wear a cap and gown, and march in order to receive his diploma. As I got to know this shy and wonderful man, he told me that he didn't go through the graduation ceremony when he graduated from the academy, either.

When he graduated from the eighth grade, his mother was his teacher, and the family lived in Brattleboro, Vermont. Ed was the only eighth grader and he was very bashful. The church members came to see their only graduate and the school play. However, Ed was up in the Vermont hills riding his bike and laughing. He had 'stood them up'. The pastor and two of the students tried in vain to persuade him to return to the church. Needless to say, when he did return after everyone had gone home, his mother-teacher grounded him and his bike for a while.

Chapter Twenty-Two

Several months before we moved to California, I noticed that I seemed to be getting weaker much too fast, and my back was hurting more that it ever did before when I walked. Panic swept over me. *"Lord, I'm happily married now, aren't I supposed to be getting stronger instead of weaker?"* Tears of frustration welled up in my eyes. *"God, are You angry with me because I lost my temper at the time of my wedding?"* I pleaded for forgiveness. I had reasoned, didn't I have a right to get angry? After all, other people got angry, and they seemed to think it was okay to get angry. Everyone always said I took life patiently. I hadn't realized at the time that it was the devil who had caused me to lose my temper. I should have prayed about it then, but I just didn't think. It took a couple of years to feel forgiven by God and the one whom I had hurt.

Soon after we arrived in Loma Linda, I decided to see a doctor at Loma Linda University Medical Center. Was there something else wrong other than Muscular Dystrophy? Doctor Miller told me that I would indeed get weaker, and one day I would have to resort to using the wheelchair *all the time* in order to take the strain off my back. It slowly hit me that one day I might not be able to walk at all! I was fighting to keep it from ever happening, or at least pushing that day as far into the future as possible.

I had known for many years that I should not gain any weight, because it would make it difficult to walk and move about if I did. However, my weight stayed fairly stable until I got married. I was enjoying the adventure in cooking for my husband so much that I gained a few pounds too many and thought maybe that could be causing my back to hurt. I didn't know very much about how to count calories or how hard it can be to lose even one pound and keep it off. For some reason, I thought that one could lose at least two or three pounds per day.

It was difficult for me to take walks outdoors to get some exercise, so Ed bought a three-wheeler bike for me after we had moved out west. With gritted teeth, I fought to keep what muscle tone I had left, but at the same time, I realized that as time passed, these muscles would grow weaker and weaker, too. I had some exercises I did on the living room floor, but I hated doing them and only did them in spells. I was fighting against myself.

One night as Ed was helping me walk to the bedroom I said angrily, "I hope I die by the time I'm forty years old; I've had enough!"

My bitter words nearly broke Ed's heart. We had not been married for a whole year yet. I wasn't thinking of him at all; I was only thinking of myself. In a broken voice he said he didn't want to lose his wife after only a few short years together.

Oh, how I wanted to take back what I had said. I wasn't angry at him; I was angry at the muscular dystrophy, and the way it was ruling my life. It was slowly taking away some of my independence. It was strenuous to do many of the things now that I used to be able to do with ease.

"I'm sorry honey, I didn't mean to hurt you," I said remorsefully.

"Honey, I know it's hard for you to walk, but I can't see you ever giving up. I think you will crawl if it ever comes to it."

"Crawl, you can't be serious!?" I said, but I knew that he was.

I didn't realize how true that statement was until three years later when it became possible for my mother-in-law to move next door to us. Ed went back to Michigan for two weeks to help her move. While he was gone, there were strawberries to pick, new fruit trees to water, and tomatoes to weed.

Peggy Ann came over to pick the strawberries, and I scooted on the ground to pick some, too. After that, I got up early one morning and scooted myself to the water faucet and turned it on. Then I scooted and crawled some more to water all the new fruit trees and strawberry plants. When that was done, I weeded the tomatoes. It was noon by the time I had finished my chores, and I went back into the house a very tired, but happy woman. I was pleased with myself for what I had been able to accomplish.

After nearly a year, I was so tired of struggling to get from room to room that I reluctantly asked Ed to bring the wheelchair in from the trunk of the car. We kept it there for whenever we went shopping and to church. I didn't want to *see* it any more than I had to.

I used the wheelchair in the house for one week. It was an exhausting week! I had removed the foot rests, and used my feet as well as the rings on the wheels to move about. When I went to the kitchen, I moved from the wheelchair to my kitchen stool which was higher, and I did the work I needed to do seated on it. In the living room, I moved again from the wheelchair to my rocker-recliner several times each day, and so on. At the end of the week I pleaded, "Lord, I'm going to fight this thing. I don't know how, but please help me."

The wheelchair went back into the trunk of the car. I prayed for strength from day to day. I had forgotten that I could take this problem to God, but from then on, I talked to God all day long. I didn't have all the answers, but I had peace. From time to time, other questions came up and God answered them.

I was having a hard time believing that the reason my back was hurting so much was the four or five pounds I had gained. I tried to lose them, but it seemed to be in vain. Shortly after we had been married three years, the pain became so unbearable that I just sat down in my special place and poured my heart out to God with tears rolling down my cheeks.

"Lord, my back hurts so much now and I can hardly take it any more. The doctors don't seem to know what the problem is, but You do Lord. Please show me what the cause is and what to do about it. Amen."

I began to notice that whenever I walked in the house, I was holding onto both sides of the hallway, and to get around the rest of the house, I would bend over and hold onto both my knees and maneuver about that way. It was wearing me out.

As I rose from my special place, I reached over to the corner of the bed, then reached for the door frame to pull myself into a standing position. One step at a time, I slowly began to walk, being cautious so I wouldn't fall. As I came to the bathroom door, my eyes caught a glimpse of the bathroom scale, sending a reminder to my brain. "You haven't weighed yourself in a year—you had better do it now!"

I placed the scale in position and stepped on it. I wasn't prepared at all for what I saw. I knew some of my clothes felt snug, but I blamed it on the dryer for shrinking them. The scale told me I had gained fifteen pounds in my three short years of marriage, and *that* was the reason my back was hurting so much!

I didn't know how to count calories, but at that moment I remembered something I had heard my mother say a number of times, "A thousand calories a day and one can lose weight." Then I thought back to what she had said to eat in order to do that. "Boiled eggs, grape-fruit...."

Well, we didn't have any grape-fruit in the house, but we had plenty of canned apricots with hardly any sugar in them. So I decided I would have a boiled egg and a dish of apricots for dinner.

When I needed to know how many calories there were in something, I would ask Ed; after all, he knew a lot about that sort of thing. He warned me that the first few pounds would come off easily, then it would be slow coming off. I lost the first five pounds in less than three weeks, and I was real pleased. At last my back wasn't hurting nearly as bad when I walked as it did before, and I wasn't getting as tired as I had been just doing a simple task such as writing a letter to my parents, sewing, or washing a few dishes.

Christmas came about six weeks after I started my dieting. On Christmas morning, Ed pulled his presents for me out from under his side of the bed and handed me one at a time, still 'wrapped' in the brown paper bags from the store. In one of those brown bags was a small pocket-size calorie counter. I really laughed when I pulled it out of the bag.

"I thought you could use it when you want to know how many calories are in something," he said with a smile.

"That's great, I like it! It will be much easier to carry around than your big green nutrition book."

By the end of six months, I had lost a total of eighteen pounds. It finally came to me that God wasn't punishing me because I had lost my temper at the time of my wedding. He loved me, no matter what. It's the devil who wants people to think God is unmerciful.

Now, I had to be careful not to gain any of it back. I was getting around much better and I hoped I would soon be able to walk down the hallway without holding onto either side. But that didn't happen, which left me a little discouraged.

I continued my regular visits to the Muscular Dystrophy clinic at the Medical Center for a while. During one of those visits they asked me if there was anything I needed which would help make my life a little bit better. For a long while Ed and I had been looking in different department stores for a stool with rollers on it to help make it easier for me in the kitchen. I was using the stool I had before I was married, but it didn't have rollers, and I wished the seat was a little bigger and the foot rest a little higher. It had served me well before, because I had been stronger. But now I needed one that was made differently.

I told the people at the clinic about my 'dream chair' and the features it would have. They, too, thought it was a dream chair. It just didn't exist.

Ed thought about putting rollers on a commercial stool from the department store, but then the seat would be too high. There were various other problems if we would buy a commercial stool, also.

Several weeks later, the phone rang. It was Mr. Martin. He was in charge of helping Muscular Dystrophy patients get a wheel-chair, crutches, and other things they might need to make life easier.

"I understand you need a wheelchair?"

"No," I replied. "I have a wheelchair. What I'd like is a stool to get around in my kitchen instead of the stool I have now, which I have to slide across the floor." I told him more about my 'dream chair' which I said didn't exist.

"No, that's easy. We can get it from office supplies," he said.

"You're kidding?!" I was getting very excited.

Mr. Martin said he would be over in a few minutes and show me a picture. It had five rollers so it wouldn't tip over very easily, and the seat and foot rest were adjustable without doing anything major. The Muscular Dystrophy Association couldn't buy it for me, because they had a shortage of funds; but I was able to buy it at a discount price.

My dream chair had become a reality. As time moved on, I had to depend on it more and more until one day, it became my 'wheelchair' in the house.

I had always been thankful that the Muscular Dystrophy had not disfigured my face, and that my arms and legs grew normally without being twisted in some way. Except for my swaying back when I stood up or walked, no one knew or could tell I had M.D. when I was sitting down. I appeared normal.

When I first started using the wheelchair when we went to church, I felt like I wanted to become invisible. I didn't want to be noticed and I just couldn't be 'me' in the wheelchair. Oh, how I longed to walk in and out of the church, but it was too much of a strain on my back. I got tired of the 'kind words' from some of the senior citizens when I was walking. They meant well, but I didn't need to be reminded.

One day, after several years of using it at church, I decided to come to terms with 'the thing'. I like to keep my wheelchair as clean as possible and as I was cleaning it, I was thinking, "You're part of my life, and as much as I don't like you, we're going to have to get along." "Lord, this wheelchair is going to be with me until the day I die; please help me to 'be me' in it." I know the Lord heard my prayer, because soon afterward it didn't bother me as much, and I could be myself.

With Sharon living two thousand miles away now, I had no one to help me alter my dresses when I made them. It was very discouraging because I did want a new dress every now and then, and I still made them. NO way could I go out and buy one and have it fit comfortably, much less look right. I knew I was on my own now and had it all to do myself. Peggy Ann never learned how to sew, so she wasn't much help, although she did try once. Even Ed tried to help me. He could put perms in my hair (and I always cut his), but in helping me alter a dress, he had a hard time understanding what I wanted done. I think I was hoping he could work a miracle and make me stand straight! However, that didn't happen, either.

I was almost finished with a dress I was making. I had altered it where I thought was the right place by basting it. Now I had to try it on and look in a full-length mirror. Taking the mirror from the wall, I leaned it up against the bed in the guest room. I moved away a few feet and said a prayer, then stood up in a door way so I would have something to hold on to for balance. I noticed the basted alterations weren't too far off.

I continued to stand there a few minutes longer, with a tear or two blurring my vision. I bit my lower lip as I thought about Ed, and his wonderful unending love for me. *"Nancy, you are one very lucky woman to have a tender loving husband like Ed, even if your body is not like Miss America."* A smile came across my lips. God had sent me a very extraordinary man, indeed!

A few days later when I was nestled in Ed's arms, I told him about the dress and what I had thought as I looked in the full length mirror that day.

"I love you, honey, for loving me just the way I am," I said with mist in my eyes. I felt his arms gently squeeze me.

Chapter Twenty-Three

I continued to ask God for strength each day, and for His Divine healing. I craved for answers to my questions, all the while knowing we are supposed to be happy and content with what we have, whether it be clothes, home, food, health, or whatever. I didn't dwell on the fact that my clothes didn't fit me as nicely as others did. I knew I had done my best with the knowledge I had.

I had been reading MINISTRY OF HEALING and STEPS TO CHRIST—not only once, but a number of times. There was nothing I had done to cause the M.D. A lot of people brought their illness on themselves by the eating habits, smoking, and drinking. However, I didn't do any of these things, so why was this my cross to bear?

I carefully studied every text in the Bible concerning Divine healing, and heard something on the radio about it, too. I read other books on Divine healing. Everything I read was backed by texts from the Bible.

Everything I read seemed to be saying that all I had to do to be healed was ask God for healing and believe that I would be made whole; and when I was healed, it would bring glory to God. It all sounded so convincing, but a lot of questions came up, too—questions that had no answers. I knew sickness was of the devil, and I also knew God was in control. I just needed to be patient and let the Lord lead me.

Was it possible that I could be completely healed now if I sincerely believed? I wondered if it would happen in just a moment, or if it would happen over a period of years. After all, I didn't become the way I was over night. Maybe now I was ready to be healed, and wasn't when I was fifteen. I recalled it had taken Moses forty years to be prepared to lead the Children of Israel.

I wanted very much to be healed, and what a ministry this would be for God's glory. I began to believe I would be healed—I even had dreams at night of me jumping out of bed and *running* to the full length mirror in the bathroom and standing beautifully straight in front of it! I held onto what the Bible said, and trusted in God each passing day.

I always knew that when we asked God for something, we were to believe He had done His part, and we had to do our part by acting on it in faith. So, I decided I wanted to make a couple of dresses, but this time they would be made 'normal' with no alterations. I wanted to make them just like the pattern. In fact, "I'm going to make them in a style I haven't been able to wear for almost twenty years," I told myself.

When I called Peggy Ann on the telephone, she agreed to take me shopping. I was really on cloud nine! As I sat down at the dining room table with the material and pattern laid out before me, I dared not to cut one inch of cloth until I had prayed. *"Lord, I believe You have healed me, and I'm acting in faith by making these dresses to wear."* I couldn't picture it any other way. I made three dresses, and hung them in the closet awaiting 'the day' when I would need them.

We were leaving for vacation back east to see my parents. I packed two of the dresses to show Mom. I didn't tell her the full story behind the dresses for fear she might say something to discourage me. She told me for the first time I could remember that she had asked the Lord many times to help me become physically stronger. The Lord used Mom in a special way; she asked me where in the Bible was the text: "To the law and to the testimony: If they speak not according to this word, it is because there is no light in them." (Isaiah 8:20) I found the text for her in the concordance at the back of the Bible.

I thought about that text for weeks afterward. As I was rolling out a pie crust one Friday after we returned home from vacation, tears were coming down in big drops, and splattered into my pie crust. *"God, I hate You. Why aren't You helping me get stronger?"* I had been having a hard time getting out of the bathtub for the past year or so, and I always asked God to help me so I wouldn't fall. It hurts me deeply to think of it now, but I was angry with God. At the same time, I didn't want to let go of His love for me. *"How can someone love and hate God at the same time?"* I wondered. It does happen.

I had been trying to ride my three-wheeler as often as I could for exercise, but that wasn't enough. I wanted to do more walking and prayed about it asking God how I could do that. One morning, as I walked down the hallway to the kitchen, it came to me. *"Why not walk up and down the hallway a number of times each morning?"* At first, it was difficult to make even one round-trip, but I was determined to get stronger if I could. It took five minutes to make one round-trip; a distance that took Ed or anyone else only about five seconds to travel. As I walked along, I sang out loud to myself, "Precious Lord, take my hand...I am weak, but Thou art strong." Also, I sang, "I Saw A Man" by Arthur Smith, and many other songs that came to my mind which lifted me up the Lord.

All winter long I kept up the round-trips, working hard at it until I was making as many as fifteen round-trips each day, except on the week-ends when I would rest. When summer came my hands became warm and sweaty, and would slide down the walls instead of helping to hold me up. Because of this problem, I didn't do any walking during the summer months for fear of falling, but I was anxiously looking forward to winter when my hands were cool and only slightly moist, giving me a good grip on the walls in the hallway.

In the meantime, something was happening to me; the Lord was helping me to realize I could be wearing the three dresses I made. *"I'm always sitting down in the wheelchair whenever I go places, and I'm sitting in the pew at church, so why not wear them. You look normal sitting down, don't you?"* I asked myself. While the burden of being more and more dependent of the wheelchair was crushing down on me, the burden of worrying how I looked standing up was being taken away.

Slowly, I was being healed. *Really* healed! Not the physical healing I had been hoping for, but something better; a spiritual and mental healing. I was where I could best serve Him, and that was all that mattered.

I loved wearing the new dresses so much that I decided to 'un-alter' the other dresses in my closet if I could. September, 1984, rolled around on the calendar, and an exciting thought popped into my head. *"I will soon be forty years old—why not celebrate it by going out and buying a new dress!"*

I could hardly wait to tell Peggy Ann, because I wanted my sister to go with me. "Now I don't want to go to K-Mart. I want to go to a place like MERVYN'S," I said.

I was bursting with excitement when Peggy Ann arrived a few days later. Ed gave me plenty of money—we knew dresses cost a lot more than they did many years ago. Peggy Ann pushed the wheelchair through the front door of MERVYN'S then over to the ladies' section of the store. There, on a rack in plain view was a pretty red dress with a double peplum. I knew right away that it was the dress I wanted, but I wondered if I should get a red dress. When I looked at it more closely, I noticed it just happened to be in my size, too!

"I wonder if the Lord put it here for a reason," I asked myself, remembering the pretty red dress I had twenty years earlier.

We found another dress of the same style in a different color, but were unable to find one in my size. Peggy Ann suggested I try on both dresses, even if the other one was not the right size, to see how they looked. We concluded the red one was indeed the one that looked the best on me. I hugged my package after we paid for it, like a little child with a brand new toy. It was the first dress I had bought in over fifteen years!

The second year of walking up and down the hallway each morning was more difficult. It was harder rising up from the corner of the bed, and using the door frame to pull myself up, too. The type of M.D. I have is Limb/Girdle. I could feel the girdle area was getting weaker. That's why I couldn't get up from the floor, or get out of the bathtub by myself any more, also. I didn't want to fall flat on my face when Ed was not around. I didn't want to give up my walking exercises either, but after the second winter, I had to.

So that I could be independent when I was caring for my personal needs, we had a shower installed, and I had a seat to sit on in the tub.

Not knowing what the future would hold for me, I learned to live one day at a time, trusting in the Lord to give the strength I would need for whatever might come my way.

Sometimes when I am watching someone on TV who is in a wheelchair or has to walk with crutches I am saddened by their need to deny the truth when they say they had no trouble accepting their disability. I can't help thinking to myself how phony it sounds.

No one can accept a disability that easily. Losing the use of any part of ones body is like losing a loved one. There is a time of grieving. Sometimes the grief may be longer for some than it is for others, but they do have to experience grief before they can experience healing.

As for me, my grief was in stages, but now through the Grace of our Lord Jesus Christ, I am healed.

In a memoir my mother wrote in 1981, she said these words:

"When our son, Bobby, died we thought the world had ended, but we had to remember we had other children to love. Then, when we learned Nancy had M.D., we thought it was more than we could bear. But the Lord said that He would never put on us more than we can bear. That helped us through the two worst tragedies of our lives. We are so glad that Nancy's faith and trust in God is helping her bear what we thought was unbearable."

Chapter Twenty-Four

Being handicapped sometimes has its advantages along with the frustrating disadvantages. Once in a while it's all wrapped up into one package. Since I can no longer walk, I use the wheelchair whenever I go anywhere, and I use my 'dream stool' with the rollers to get around in the house, because it is much smaller and sits higher up.

It's very easy for me to tell who is uncomfortable with a wheelchair, and who isn't. Those who are uncomfortable pretend they don't see me and talk to the one pushing my wheelchair, as if I'm retarded, or deaf. Lots of people make the mistake, unintentionally, of standing to my side which tires my neck, because then I not only have to turn my head—I also have to look up as well. I wish they would stand in front of me, and since they are stronger, bend down to my eye level.

I always enjoy it when I have to fly in an airplane; they tend to all my needs and still make me feel as if I'm normal.

It was May, 1985, and I was flying home to spend three weeks with my parents in West Virginia. I was proud that I had bought my super-saver ticket several months before. Unfortunately, I was disappointed with the seat I had been assigned to. I always try to get a window seat just behind the partition separating the first-class section from the rest of the plane, (which I've now learned is called a 'bulkhead'.) There is more leg room and it is closer and more accessible to the lavatory in case I need to make use of it. However, this time I was given an aisle seat in row 18.

"That man wasn't listening," I fumed. *"Here I am in row 18, and what if I...."* My hips were a little sore from rubbing the seats as they wheeled me in an aisle chair down the narrow aisle-way to my seat. Although I was in a non-smoking section, I was disgusted at how the smoke from the smoking section was drifting toward those of us who hate the stench of it.

Whenever I flew, I tried to plan it so I wouldn't need to use the tiny lavatory before I arrived at my destination by drinking no water and very little other liquids. But this time things weren't working out the way I had planned. While I was eating my breakfast, a terrible urge and uncomfortable feeling came over me. I tried to make it go away, but couldn't, and I was a little thirsty, too. *"What am I going to do? It's really a long way to the lavatory in the front of the plane. And it's not much closer to the one in the back, either."* I sat there pondering my dilemma. *"I could hold it, but I'd be really miserable for a very long time, because I'm only a little more than an hour into my flight, and there won't be enough time in Chicago."*

Since I could no longer walk, I pondered some more about what to do. If I was nearer to the first class section, I could hold onto my knees and maneuver myself sideways; besides, I wouldn't have far to go and the aisle is wider in the first class section.

I wondered if they kept an aisle-chair on board that I wasn't aware of, in case of an emergency such as mine. I certainly hoped so, because I had decided to ask a female flight attendant if they had any accommodations on board to help a handicapped person to the lavatory.

"Let me see if there is an aisle-chair on board," she replied.

I doubted that there was, but I was hoping for a miracle and that maybe I was wrong.

She returned in a little bit and said, "Sorry, we don't have an aisle-chair for safety reasons in case someone might get hurt. Maybe I can help you; can you hold on to me?"

"No, I'm afraid that won't work. I have M.D. which weakens the muscles, and I can't walk anymore." I knew if I held on to her, I'd land on the floor of the plane for sure. "That's O.K.," I said. "I'll just wait."

I knew if I waited until I got to the O'Hare airport in Chicago, I would have only forty-five minutes there after my plane landed (if it wasn't late), and that I would be the last one off the plane. Sometimes I had to wait for fifteen or twenty minutes before someone would come with an aisle-chair and a wheelchair besides, to take me off the plane. That wouldn't leave any time to take care of the urgent matter at hand.

"No, let's see what we can do," said the flight attendant. "How much do you weigh? Are you pregnant?" After she asked me a few other questions, I said, "It's O.K.; I'll wait. Thank-you for trying, anyway."

The flight attendant was kind and sincerely wanted to help, and she didn't give up easily.

"Suppose two of us carried you?"

I couldn't believe my ears and smiled, "You're kidding?"

"No. Suppose the male flight attendant gets hold of you on one side, and I take hold of the other side, and help you?"

"I'm afraid when you carry me you are my support. My legs are like jelly," I said.

"Then, suppose he carries you under your arms, and I'll carry your legs?"

I could see she wasn't going to give up on me. Very, very reluctantly, I agreed. The male flight attendant got under my arms from behind, and the female attendant picked up my legs. Down the aisle we went—backward. All I could do was grin at my predicament. Some of the other passengers looked our way and smiled. I could tell they were all understanding the situation.

"Wait until I tell my husband about this," I was telling the flight attendants, "He'll get a real bang out of it."

As we neared the rest room in the rear of the plane, the male attendant asked, "How will we get her in there?"

"just back up in there and sit her down," the female flight attendant replied.

I really had to laugh at that!

"Are you kidding?" he said, "I won't be able to get back out!"

I could tell by the way he was holding me that I was getting heavy. As we got to the door of the lavatory, they still weren't sure how to help me inside.

"Is it O.K. if I sit you down on the floor a minute?" the male flight attendant asked.

"Sure!" I replied, feeling a little relief, because my arms were hurting a wee-bit. So there I was, sitting on the *floor* of the airplane, thousands of feet up in the air!

I noticed a bench behind me that the flight attendants use during take-off and landing.

"Why not lift me up on that bench, and I can make it in there on my own?" I asked.

"Are you sure?"

"Yup! Just lift me up there."

After I was pulled to my feet, I put my hands on my knees and slowly made it to my destination—the lavatory. When I got in I turned myself around, sat down, and locked the door.

"Lord, I'm thankful for caring people, but does it have to be so embarrassing sometimes?"

It was frustrating to find that my terrible urge was much greater than my need. I tried to rid myself of the uncomfortable feeling, but it was almost in vain. However, I did feel some better after a while, so it wasn't all for nothing. When I was through, I washed my hands, checked my clothing twice to make sure everything was in proper order, and opened the door. I was still sitting on the facility.

The male flight attendant wasn't too far away. After all, how far could he go 36,000 feet in the air. I reached out my hand to his.

"Pull," I said. Rising to my feet, I put my hands on my knees again, and inched my way back to the flight attendants' bench.

"Ready?" I was asked after I reached the bench.

"I guess so," I replied shyly.

"Here we go again," I thought. I could feel my cheeks blushing beet-red! The female attendant held my legs, and the male attendant held me under the arms as they carried me back down the aisle. There were more smiles as we passed by the other passengers. Once back in my seat I thanked the attendants for their care and help.

When the plane* landed in Chicago, I got a pat on the shoulder from some of the passengers as they walked off the plane. Some of them said they thought I was brave, thinking maybe I had never flown before.

I thought, *"This has to be the most embarrassing time of my life!"*

·——————————————————·

When I started writing my autobiography, I knew that I might lose one of my parents before they would have a chance to see it in print. So every summer when I went to see them, I would tell them or read to them some of the stories I had written. In turn, they told me some stories about myself which I had forgotten.

This visit would be over in a few short days, and then I would have to go back home to California. I sat on Dad's bed beside him and we talked. I put my arm around his shoulder, with my hand hanging over the other shoulder. His body was crippled with rheumatoid arthritis which he had suffered with for the last fifteen (or so) years. Most of his joints were frozen tight and were

---

*   *Airplanes are now being built to meet the needs of the handicapped.*

hard to move, but he tried his best to reach up and take my hand in his. A little frustrated, he said, "I can't even take hold of your hand." I gave him a tender hug.

As I sat there with my arm around my dear father, I wondered if I would ever have another moment like this. A few days later I went into his bedroom in the wee hours of the morning to have prayer with my parents, and give them a big hug and kiss before leaving for the airport. As I reached down to give Dad his hug and kiss, I said cheerfully, "I'll see ya next summer, Pop!"

He didn't say anything.

·_____·

Ever since we were married, Ed had wanted to take me to the New England States and show me the places where he grew up as a child, but we wondered if we could afford to make such a long trip. A month before our eighth wedding anniversary he suggested we go to the New England States. It turned out to be the honeymoon we hadn't had. On our way, we stopped at Niagara Falls, and went over into Canada for one night, then we went on to make a tour of New England. On our way back to California, we stopped over in West Virginia to help Dad celebrate his 83rd birthday.

In late February I received a phone call from Sharon. She had just called Mom and said that Dad was taken back to the hospital only a few minutes earlier. Sharon said I had better come home as soon as possible.

When we all arrived at the hospital 48 hours later, Dad said he had told Mom, "Nancy will be here even if she has to walk to get here." We all laughed. Dad still had his sense of humor.

I spent most of the day on Friday at the hospital. That night, before leaving Dad's side, I longed to give him another hug, but the side rails were in my way. None of us thought of letting them down until later. I knew family members would be in during the week-end, and there might not be another opportunity to be with Dad. A part of me didn't want to say 'good-bye', but another part of me knew he had suffered enough. He was kidding me earlier in the day; "Ed'll get a divorce from you if you stay away from him four weeks." I had wondered how he knew.

"No he won't, Pop!" "He's a good ol' boy like you always say," I said with all the enthusiasm I could muster so I wouldn't break.

I took his hand in mine and asked God for strength to say what I wanted to say to him. I had tried a little earlier, but didn't make it. I think Dad sensed what I might be trying to say, and he asked for a nurse.

There were times when we had talked about Heaven and all the joys we would share; like the two of us would be strong again, and *we would run together!*

"Daddy..I love you. And..and..when Jesus comes, we will run together." His hearing was failing, and I wondered if he really heard me, because he said nothing; he only turned his head. I realized later Dad did hear me and didn't say anything because he knew he couldn't without breaking down.

Sharon was Daddy's favorite singer, and I had been praying that she would have an opportunity to sing some of his favorite hymns before the end came for him. Sunday night while I prayed again, He answered. She sang his favorites, and new ones, too. God also performed another miracle. Dad closed his mouth and was breathing through his nose for the first time in months. "God filled my cup to over-flowing," Dad was singing along with her! For an hour and a half they sang together.

On March 4, 1986, Dad fell asleep in Jesus.

Chapter Twenty-Five

Sometimes I had wondered how it would have been if I had not let Muscular Dystrophy bother me in the least, and zipped through my life as a happy person all the time. As I reflect back, it was good I had my trials and tears, so that I would be better able to understand others who suffer hurt and misery.

Now that I had won my battle, with God leading me each step of the way in my life, I was ready and willing to go out and speak. However, I didn't know how I could get started in giving my ministry to the public. I took it to God in prayer. As I was busy one day making bread, the answer came to me in a 'still, small voice'.

"Volunteer to be a Sabbath School Superintendent at Mentone."

"Okay Lord, that's just what I'll do!" I prayed silently.

In a few months, a sheet of paper was passed to each church member with a space to mark for whatever office in the church the member might desire to serve in. I had worked in the Kindergarten division for several years, and as a receptionist (greeter) for a couple of years. This time I marked the space for 'Sabbath School Superintendent'. I had butterflies in my stomach as I did it, and thought to myself, *"Are you sure you want to do this, Nancy?"* Doubts were flooding my mind.

"Yes! The devil isn't going to win this one."

I knew there would be more than one Sabbath School Superintendent, therefore, I would be up front only one Sabbath of each month.

I prayed many times in the coming weeks as I prepared my first program.

"Sharon, since you and Mom are coming to California to help Ed and me celebrate our tenth wedding anniversary, would you be willing to give a mini concert for my first Sabbath as a superintendent?" I bubbled excitedly as I talked long distance to my sister.

I wanted to share my feelings about God's leading in my life, and wondered if I would be able to get my church family to understand how I felt inside.

It was embarrassing as Ed wheeled me up the two steps at the front of the church with all eyes focused on us. Also, I feared that people might have a hard time understanding my sometimes faltering speech. Ed handed me the microphone, and I read to the Sabbath School thoughts I had written down just for this occasion:

Many years ago, "O Lord," I prayed,
"I'll go and speak for You
But first make me strong."

"It doesn't matter it you're weak or strong,
It's what's in your heart that counts," He said.
"O.K. Lord," I prayed that day, "You lead the way."

As I thought about my desire,
"O Lord," I panicked again.
"What about my speech?" I asked.

"It's not perfect, You know.
Oh, what shall I do?" I mumbled with despair.
"Go and speak the loving words," He said,
"And leave the rest up to Me."

"Now Lord, what about my hearing?
It, too, is far from perfect, You know.
What if I should make a blunder
And give some wrong answer, because I misunderstood?"

"Don't worry, my child.
You just do your best," He said,
"And leave the rest up to Me."

"But Lord, what about the wheelchair?
It's so big and bulky. You see,
It takes up lots of room besides.

"I feel a little uncomfortable when going up steps
With so many people to see.
You know how I like to be in control,
With all four wheels on the ground."

"My child, My child," He scolded tenderly.
"You worry much too much.
I use all kinds of people, dear,
To be My helpers, you see.
You just smile and leave the rest up to Me."

"Thank you Lord, for muscular dystrophy,
And all the tears and trials I've suffered.
Because, one day soon
When we see that small dark cloud in the sky,
You have come to take us home.

"I shall rise from this chair,
Leaping and running to meet my Lord,
And say, 'Thank you Lord, for giving Your life
That we may dwell with You for eternity.'"

And He said unto me, My grace is sufficient for thee: for my strength is made perfect in weakness. Most gladly, therefore, will I rather glory in my infirmities, that the power of Christ may rest upon me. II Corinthians 12:9

THE END

From Tears to Triumph